# *Raising*
# RESILIENT &
# COMPASSIONATE
# *Children*

I highly recommend *Raising Resilient and Compassionate Children*. The authors present all the important information about the Aware Parenting approach in a single, very readable, book. They explain how to offer children empathy, unconditional love, and full acceptance of their emotions. In addition, they clearly describe the underlying reasons for behaviour problems and suggest many alternatives to punishments and rewards.

To supplement the theory, the book includes rich examples illustrating typical scenarios which parents might encounter with their children (some of which are real-life experiences with the authors' own children). These examples and anecdotes provide parents with practical tools to cope successfully with challenging situations, and they also help to explain children's behaviour.

I was especially touched by the deep compassion for parents, which shines through on every page. The authors fully understand why it's sometimes hard for parents to respond patiently and lovingly to their children. In the final section called 'Reparenting Ourselves', they offer helpful exercises for parents to explore their own childhood and heal from their own early wounds.

~ Aletha Solter, PhD., Founder of Aware Parenting


*Raising Resilient and Compassionate Children* is not just for parents. This is for anyone who would like to see a brighter future for the human race. It is the ultimate parenting tool kit that has the potential to be life changing.

This book is emotionally engaging and jam packed with practical advice and it is a must read for anyone who finds parenting challenging ... i.e. all of us!

~ Hugh van Cuylenburg, Founder – The Resilience Project

*Raising Resilient and Compassionate Children* is the book we have all been waiting for. The pages are filled with wisdom and most importantly practical ways to live our parenting values. These words have the power to not only change your family, but the world. A must read for all parents and educators.

~ Fleur Wood, CEO South Pacific Private

This book is life changing. Lael and Marion beautifully share how to raise compassionate and resilient children, while inviting the reader to show themselves so much compassion in the process. Reading this book feels like receiving a big warm hug – you are being held and supported while learning how to support your children. It is full of tangible examples of specific scenarios that commonly play out between parent and child and how to work through them.

It is not just providing scripts though, it speaks to the importance of doing the work on yourself as a parent, healing your own childhood wounds, giving yourself the love, listening and compassion you may not have received as a child, in order to be able to be fully present while holding space for your children – while also giving you permission to put down the guilt sticks when you don't have the capacity to do so. If every parent read this book, the world would be a very different place.

~ Katie Parker – Social Worker, Counsellor, Parenting Educator

Published in Australia by
Wise Women Publishing
PO Box 256, Doreen, VIC 3754
info@wisewomenpublishing.au
www.wisewomenpublishing.au

First published in Australia 2022

Copyright © Lael Stone and Marion Rose 2022

All rights reserved. No part of this publication may be reproduced, stored in a retrieval system, or transmitted, in any form or by any means without the prior written permission of the publisher, nor be otherwise circulated in any form of binding or cover other than that in which it is published and without a similar condition being imposed on the subsequent purchaser.

National Library of Australia Cataloguing in Publication entry

 A catalogue record for this book is available from the National Library of Australia

ISBN: 978-0-6455515-3-2 (paperback)
ISBN: 978-0-6455515-4-9 (hardback)
ISBN: 978-0-6455515-5-6 (epub)

Cover layout and design by Mike Gaal - www.gaal.com.au
Book design by Mike Gaal - www.gaal.com.au
Typesetting by Sophie White Design - www.sophiewhite.com.au
Printed by Ingram Spark

All care has been taken in the preparation of the information herein, but no responsibility can be accepted by the publisher or author for any damages resulting from the misinterpretation of this work. All contact details given in this book were current at the time of publication, but are subject to change.

The advice given in this book is based on the experience of the individuals. Professionals should be consulted for individual problems. The author and publisher shall not be responsible for any person with regard to any loss or damage caused directly or indirectly by the information in this book.

**Today, and every day, we acknowledge the Traditional Custodians of this land where we live and work, the Arakwal people, the Minjungbal people and the Widjabul people of the Bundjalung Nation and the Wadawurrung people who are part of the Kulin Nation. We pay our respects to elders past, present and emerging. We acknowledge and recognise their resilience, heritage and their ongoing relationship as traditional owners of the land. We recognise the immense privilege it is to live, work and grow on this stolen land.**

# *Raising* RESILIENT & COMPASSIONATE *Children*

A parenting guide to understanding behaviour, feelings and relationships

Lael Stone and
Marion Rose, PhD

# Dedication

**Marion says:**

I'm so grateful to Aletha Solter, PhD., for Aware Parenting. It has profoundly affected my life in so many ways, particularly my family, my calling and my community.

Thank you to my daughter, who invited me on the Aware Parenting journey in the first place, and to my son, who helped me embody and understand it even more deeply. I so appreciate you both showing me so clearly what a huge difference Aware Parenting makes for children and for being the inspiration for wanting to help spread Aware Parenting far and wide.

I am forever honoured to have walked beside parents with Aware Parenting since 2005. Thank you to each and every one of you for sharing your experiences and feelings and for being a part of the Aware Parenting family.

Last but not least, all my loving appreciation to my parents, who always supported me to walk the path less travelled.

**Lael says:**

I have deep gratitude to Aletha Solter, PhD., and all those that have walked before me who have championed connection and seeing the heart of the child. Thank you to my parents for loving me deeply and always standing in my corner, encouraging me to follow whatever my heart desired. I am grateful to them for reflecting that I am and always will be enough.

Thank you to the thousands of parents who have shared their stories with me and trusted me with their hearts.

My darling children, all three of you have brought me gifts beyond my wildest dreams – you have allowed me to learn and grow, and you show me each day what it is to live connected to your essence.

And finally, my husband Mike, together we make a hundred per cent. None of this magic is possible without you.

# Contents

| | | |
|---|---|---|
| Preface | | 10 |
| Our Parenting Journeys | | 13 |
| Marion's Aware Parenting Journey | | 14 |
| Lael's Aware Parenting Story | | 17 |
| An Invitation | | 20 |
| **Part I** | **Understanding Children's Behaviour and Feelings** | **22** |
| Chapter 1 | The Evolution of Parenting | 23 |
| Chapter 2 | Feelings and Behaviour | 29 |
| Chapter 3 | Understanding Children's Feelings | 46 |
| **Part II** | **Responses to Everyday Parenting Challenges** | **70** |
| Chapter 4 | Not Cooperating and Not Listening | 71 |
| Chapter 5 | Feelings and Tears and Tantrums | 84 |
| Chapter 6 | Aggression and Power-over | 97 |
| Chapter 7 | Fear, Anxiety, Trust, Attachment and Separation | 121 |
| Chapter 8 | Sleep | 129 |
| Chapter 9 | Suppression and Dissociation | 148 |

| | | |
|---|---|---|
| **Part III** | **Reparenting Ourselves** | **174** |
| Chapter 10 | Repair and Compassion | 175 |
| Chapter 11 | Exploring Our Imprints | 189 |

| | |
|---|---|
| Conclusion | 208 |
| Glossary | 210 |
| Further Resources | 216 |
| Acknowledgments | 217 |
| About the Authors | 218 |

# Preface

Hello and a big warm welcome to you! As you read this book, we are so willing for you to receive an abundance of empathy, information and support for your own unique parenting path. Through our own experiences of the challenges of parenting, we have developed a deep compassion for ourselves and all parents. We would love to offer that same quality of empathy and unconditional love to you, knowing that each of us is doing the utmost we can at any moment to be the parent we want to be.

As parents, our feelings can vary from profound love to extreme frustration. Parenting invites us not only to support our children so that they can thrive but also to explore our own conditioning, emotional hurts and imprints. If you feel uncomfortable feelings whilst you read this book, we invite you to be as compassionate as you can with yourself. Whatever the age of your child or children, and whichever your parenting style so far, each of us is being invited to have more awareness, compassion and understanding for ourselves and our child. It's never too late to change or to do things differently.

We also welcome you if you're a teacher, grandparent, carer, or involved in the lives of children in other ways. We will use the term 'parent', but we are also talking to you. You are also so welcome here.

We chose the title of this book because we want to support parents to help their children move through challenging experiences whilst being compassionate, loving and truly resilient. Resilience has become a buzz-word in parenting and is often perceived as the ability to get on with things after hard experiences without being affected by them. The Oxford English Dictionary's definition of resilience – 'the capacity to recover quickly from difficulties; toughness' – echoes that perception.

In industrialised countries, many of us grew up being praised or rewarded for being 'tough', for not showing emotion during or after challenges and for being 'brave'. Our family of origin might have taught us to 'toughen up' and 'push through' whenever something was hard, whether this was going to school or being told to just 'get over it' when we felt upset. However, many years of research into understanding trauma have shown that if children experience adversity without having the support to process the feelings related to these events, later challenges such as anxiety, depression and addictive behaviours can result.

However, in this book, we return to the etymology of the word 'resilience' – 'the act of rebounding or springing back'. This description much more deeply reflects how we see as resilience from an Aware Parenting perspective. This is a true strength, which emerges from a natural process of homeostasis. It is not a forced, hard, toughness, like a nut in a hard shell. It's more like bamboo, pushed over by a big storm, springing back up to its true and flexible strength.

Resilience is not something we make happen as parents. It's something we support to naturally happen, when we understand and trust a child's inbuilt healing processes. These include feeling the feelings caused by a challenging experience, expressing these feelings with our loving support, and coming out the other side having actually released the feelings, associated stress hormones and physical tension from their body. This means that they can really and truly move on, feeling relaxed, relieved and powerful. They can leave the past behind rather than carry it with them in an ever-bigger backpack of unexpressed feelings and unhealed trauma. This process is an innate one that we are all born with but which our cultural conditioning tries to hide away and demonise, replacing it with an 'ignore it' mentality which creates tension rather than resilience.

In this book, we offer this different understanding of resilience and the practical application of it. We're here to support you to understand a child's behaviour and feelings in relation to true resilience so that you can help them move through whatever challenges life throws their way, becoming stronger and more compassionate rather than harder and more brittle. As humans, we can retain the deep sense of presence that we see in a small child gently holding a flower and gazing at it for hours. This awareness comes from truly feeling and moving through our deepest emotions, not bypassing or ignoring them.

A child who experiences empathy from the adults around them and who also gets to express the feelings that often get in the way of them staying connected with themselves continues to be able to feel and offer compassion towards themselves, their peers, other humans and animals. This doesn't require requests of them to 'be gentle' – rather, it's something that emerges naturally within the context of this way of parenting. Every day we hear stories from parents practicing Aware Parenting, telling us about ways their children have offered empathy to their siblings, peers and adults – without taking responsibility for the feelings of others.

We are so willing for this book to help you develop deeper compassion for yourself and your child/ren or the children in your life, to give you more understanding of the causes of their behaviour (and yours) and to offer you practices for more connection, harmony and healing. From these, we trust that you will witness their true resilience and compassion like a flower in bloom.

With love,

*Marion and Lael*

xoxox

November 2022, Australia

# Our Parenting Journeys

We'd like to start by acknowledging Aletha Solter, PhD., whose first book, The Aware Baby (first edition 1984, revised edition 2001), brought a revolutionary approach to helping babies and children heal from stress and trauma – Aware Parenting – which also includes attachment-style parenting and non-punitive discipline. Her book set in motion The Aware Parenting Institute, which has become a cornerstone of conscious parenting for the twenty-first century. Aletha has published six books (translated into many different languages), and her work has reached many thousands of parents worldwide.

Aletha's work was, and is, profoundly ahead of its time, bringing new elements to the theory and practice of Attachment Parenting. Building on the foundations of sensitive attunement to our children's needs, Aletha recognised the powerful effects of connected laughter, tears, raging and body movements in helping them heal from everyday stress and trauma. Without this understanding, unexpressed feelings accumulate and cause the majority of everyday parenting challenges – including a lack of cooperation, agitation, hitting and sleep issues. With this knowledge and these practices, parents can parent non-punitively – because there is no need for punishments and rewards when we know the true causes of children's behaviour.

For both of us, Aletha's work has forged a path to understanding the deeper workings of the parent-child relationship. We are deeply grateful for her guidance and wisdom in our personal and professional lives. Much of what we share in this book is based on or inspired by Aletha's work. We encourage you to read her groundbreaking and gorgeous books to discover her work for yourself!

One of the many things we love about Aware Parenting is how inclusive it is for all families. We each came to Aletha's work from different backgrounds and circumstances, yet we both deeply value its profound impact on our lives. We trust that in reading about our different experiences, you will experience that inclusivity too.

## Marion's Aware Parenting Journey

My story spans back to my own traumatic birth. Born at thirty weeks gestation and in an incubator for five weeks, it deeply affected my childhood and teen years. At eighteen, I wanted to discover why I was the way I was and why I felt so scared so much of the time. That longing for understanding and healing took me on a long journey which led to Aware Parenting.

The path included a degree in psychology and a PhD in postnatal depression and the mother-baby relationship at The Winnicott Research Unit, Cambridge University, where I spent hundreds of hours watching videos of mothers and babies that I had recorded, millisecond by millisecond. This training in observing babies was incredibly helpful when I started practising Aware Parenting with my daughter a decade later. I then did a post-Doctoral Fellowship on infant development. But I still wanted to learn more about the impact of our childhood on our adulthood, so I trained and worked as a Psychosynthesis Psychotherapist. As part of my preparation for becoming a mother, I had ten years of weekly therapy.

I moved to Australia and was ready to have a baby with my then-husband. But I was terrified of giving birth because of my own birth. In a series of synchronicities, I discovered and trained in HypnoBirthing and went from terror to deep trust in my body and my capacity to give birth.

In 2001, while pregnant with my daughter Lana, I was looking for a parenting approach that fitted everything I had learnt in my academic and therapeutic training. Discovering Aware Parenting was a big light-bulb moment for me. It fitted with all I'd learnt about secure attachment, pre- and peri-natal psychology and trauma. It also had an amazing extra piece: babies and children can heal from painful or stressful experiences, including birth, right from their birth. I had found the missing part of the puzzle.

I had a beautiful birthing experience with my daughter and I loved practicing Aware Parenting. I became an Aware Parenting instructor when my daughter was three and gave birth to my son Sunny the following year. I'd also become a Calmbirth® instructor and used Calmbirth during his unassisted birth.

I saw huge benefits for my daughter from this approach, and even more with my son, since by the time he was born, I had been practising Aware Parenting for four and a half years and had supported many parents, so I understood the theory and practice even more deeply. I had deep confidence in it from seeing the effects it had on my daughter and on the children of my friends and clients who were practicing it. Lana and Sunny were generally calm, present and cooperative. Their bodies were relaxed. Sleep was easy. They were gentle and could concentrate for long periods. They were totally in love with each other. And I felt deeply connected with them. It wasn't easy, listening to so many feelings, but it was clearly making a huge difference to them. My experiences as a parent reassured me that Aware Parenting helps children stay deeply connected with their true presence, compassionate and calm.

However, when my daughter was eight, and my son was four, their dad and I separated, and things changed tremendously. My son and I, in particular, had lots of big feelings, and those feelings showed up in his behaviour (hitting and head-butting) and my having less emotional spaciousness to respond in the ways I knew were most helpful.

It was a really hard time. However, those experiences gave me more insight and compassion into many parents' lives. I knew firsthand what it was like to have a child who was hitting and how painful that was for me to see and respond to. I became a much more effective and empathic Aware Parenting instructor after that.

It took quite a while for me to come back to being able to help my son in his healing process. But with Aware Parenting, he did stop hitting and head-butting, and it was as if I had my lovely boy back again. Through these experiences, I've come to a deep trust in the timing of healing and have deep self-compassion. I've been a single parent since then, and I'm into alternative ways of seeing the world, as you may have guessed. My children have never been to school. And my children's dad has a partner and twins and he also became an Aware Parenting instructor in 2022.

Since 2014, I've created loads of online courses on Aware Parenting and other aspects of parenting, including our own inner reparenting and getting free from guilt. I see Aware Parenting as part of the evolution of consciousness and am passionate about this bigger cultural lens. I've also developed my work – The Marion Method for Psychospiritual Parenting, ReParenting and ReCulturing.

I met Lael in 2008 and am so grateful to be friends and colleagues with such an inspiring and powerful woman. After running workshops in Melbourne, Australia, her hometown, many years ago, we became close, leading to collaborations such as The Aware Parenting Podcast and this book. I love what Lael brings to parents worldwide and am always inspired by the relationships she has with her children. I also really enjoy that Lael and I have had such different experiences and that we bring such unique flavours and gifts to this work.

I became a Level Two Aware Parenting instructor a few years ago and am the Regional Coordinator for Australia and New Zealand. My expertise is in Aware Parenting with babies and young children, working with people who have already done a lot of inner work, and those who want to become Aware Parenting instructors or who are already Aware Parenting instructors.

My children are now young adults, and we live near Byron Bay, Australia with my Mum in our granny flat, three French Bulldogs and the wild Welcome Swallows that nest in our home!

## Lael's Aware Parenting Story

My upbringing was full of love and stability. My brothers and I benefited greatly from my mother's quest for all things conscious, and I was exposed from a young age to the concepts of self-awareness, mindfulness and spirituality.

I became a mother at twenty-five to my son Ky. I had travelled and started my own business, but I also felt this deep rumbling in my belly to have a baby. My husband Mike and I hadn't been together for very long, so when we became pregnant, it was a shock but a welcomed surprise. Without any preparation and community to show me the way, I ended up with a traumatic birth experience, a very unsettled baby and a sense of shock that stayed with me for the first year of my son's life.

As a parent, I knew what kind of family environment I wanted. One that was full of calm, beautiful surroundings and placid contented children connected and living their best creative lives. Instead, I found myself in the first few years of parenting, struggling with the current reality. We were under pressure financially. I had no community of parents to lean on, and I didn't realise at the time that I had PTSD from my son's birth. I internalised all of this to mean that I wasn't a good mother, I had no idea what I was doing and mothering was the hardest job ever. For those first few years, my beautiful husband forged a divine bond with our son and showed up in ways I couldn't.

Three years later, I gave birth to my daughter, Indi. After finally doing some birth debriefing and counselling, I made different choices, found a team to support me and had a powerful healing water birth that altered the course of my life. I fell deeply in love with my daughter, and her birth sparked a passion for helping women to have positive births.

The following year, I became a doula and a childbirth educator, and my passion for understanding trauma was sparked. I had the incredible privilege of working in birth, supporting women through grief and loss, holding space whilst they birthed their babies and listening to hundreds and hundreds of birth stories.

By the time my son was seven, I was pregnant with my third child. Planning another beautiful, peaceful birth, life had other ideas, and after a long labour and an undiagnosed breech discovery, I had an emergency Caesarean. My daughter and I both reacted badly to the anaesthetic, and she was born not breathing and was resuscitated for close to ten minutes. Her prognosis was grim; she wasn't expected to live, and if she did, she would likely have brain damage.

This was one of those life-changing moments that taught you about surrender and trust. Those early days in the hospital with my baby in the NICU taught me more about letting go than any other event in my life. I made peace with my beautiful daughter Tali and told her that I trusted whatever decision she needed to make.

After four days, she came out of the coma, and much to every doctor's surprise, there didn't seem to be any neurological damage. When she was ten days old, we took her home. After all my work, I knew that traumatic births could impact attachment and bonding and set up future patterns regarding our relationship with life. I knew my daughter and I needed to heal but wasn't sure how to do it. A friend told me about *The Aware Baby* book by Aletha Solter, and as soon as I read it, I felt like I had found the missing piece in my parenting tool kit.

I am an attachment parent. I breastfed my kids for ages, we co-slept, I wore them on my body, and I tried not to use punishments and rewards – but I didn't know what to do when they got upset. My default was to try and distract them or keep them happy. Both methods failed miserably, and I found myself exhausted trying to meet everyone's needs and living in a house with a low level of tension. Aletha's work opened up a new paradigm for me around sitting with feelings and emotions and listening and supporting the whole child. I sat my husband down, told him the concept and said, 'Let's start listening'.

The next few months could have seemed like chaos as we encouraged our children to cry and express themselves. I no longer shut down their feelings, and all three of my children started revealing the hurts they had been carrying.

The change in our family was phenomenal. Everybody started to get their needs met, my older kids stopped fighting, and that tension transitioned into a sense of ease in our home. I learnt about boundaries and limits and to take care of myself.

As I explored Aware Parenting further, I longed for a mentor or friend to discuss the changes I saw in my kids. I also needed to process the feelings that were surfacing for me. I didn't know anyone parenting this way until I found the beautiful Marion Rose, and she became a beacon of light. Her understanding and experience with Aware Parenting opened up a deeper level of awareness, and I knew that this way of parenting was so important to my work.

I became an Aware Parenting instructor, and that glorious journey opened many doors – working one-on-one with families, running workshops and taking these concepts into high schools as I worked with teens around sex education and relationship awareness. In 2021, with my co-creator Mel, we opened Woodline Primary. A revolutionary primary school set in the gorgeous Geelong Hinterland based on some of the philosophies of Aware Parenting. Our school aims to exemplify what is possible when we focus on choice, autonomy, emotional awareness and connection first. We are a school that supports feelings in children and adults, and we are working to be an example of how our education system could look when we put the child at the centre of the system.

Working with Marion has been the greatest joy, and it has been thrilling to see how our Aware Parenting Podcast has reached so many people worldwide.

I am so blessed to live on the Surf Coast in Victoria with my beautiful husband of twenty-five years and my three children (two of whom are now adults), who have all attended mainstream schools and navigated being raised with Aware Parenting in a bustling city.

# An Invitation

You've probably gathered by now that we are all about compassion and deep trust. This isn't like other parenting books. We won't be telling you that you are doing things 'wrong' and we will not tell you that you 'should' do what we say. Instead, throughout this book, we invite you to tune into yourself and listen to what fits. We're here to support you in being your own authority in parenting. That comes from you listening to yourself and what resonates for you as you read this, exploring practices that speak to you, observing how your child is before, during and after the experimenting you do, and making your conclusions and any adjustments for next time.

Aware Parenting isn't about trying to do something 'right' or 'perfectly' as that would be simply a replaying of harsh cultural conditioning. Instead, it's an ongoing deepening of understanding of the needs, feelings and behaviours of our children and ourselves and embodying that understanding in our responses to both them and to us.

What we share isn't primarily about techniques (although you'll discover tangible ways to respond to your child/ren during common parenting challenges). This work is based on relationships first and foremost – both our relationship with ourselves and with our child/ren. Whenever you're unsure of what to do, we invite you to come back to compassionate connection with yourself and your child.

Throughout the pages of this book, we will explain why children behave in certain ways and we give you lots of real-life examples, so you can see what goes on for children and us as adults.

We imagine that many of you will relate to the stories and situations we share, and you might notice judgmental thoughts about yourself when you read them. We remind you to be compassionate with yourself, seeing the information not as an opportunity for more self-judgement, but for more understanding of the 'why' behind how we react and the 'what' we can do to change our responses.

We believe that information, combined with action and willingness to create change, can help a parent shift from old patterns and conditioning into experiencing more joy and harmony in their family, with compassion and resilience at the centre.

Some of the recommendations in this book might not be suitable for children with specific medical, emotional, or psychological issues. We always advise seeking professional assistance if you are worried about your child's health or mental wellbeing. This book is not meant as a substitute for professional guidance.

We also invite you to take a look at the glossary at the back of the book if you require further explanation of some of the terms and phrases that we use.

This book came about thanks to the support and encouragement of The Aware Parenting Podcast community and the many families that we both work with, as well as our Aware Parenting instructor colleagues and others. Our raw and real podcast has spread far and wide and we have been so touched seeing Aware Parenting resonating with so many people.

Each idea is of its time, and we see that the consciousness of parents has shifted since each of us started practicing Aware Parenting, to a deep hunger and readiness for this information. We believe that Aware Parenting is on the cusp of becoming much more well-known and we see the podcast and this book as part of that process, in addition to Aletha Solter's amazing books.

This book has taken its time in being born into the world and we deeply trust that timing.

We wrote this book together, in collaboration. Perhaps you could imagine us sitting together, drinking cups of tea or smoothies (or whatever you love to drink), chatting together. Like we do on the podcast, only this time, you're sitting there with us. We are honoured to go on this journey with you. Let's begin!

# Part I
# Understanding Children's Behaviour and Feelings

*'Look behind the behaviour.'*

~ Lael

CHAPTER 1

# The Evolution of Parenting

Lael recalls a session with Sarah and John:

> *Sarah and John are sitting on my couch, clearly upset. They have come to see me because their six-year-old daughter Hannah has just had another outburst, the fifth time this week. Sarah is trying to hold back the tears: 'Why would a six-year-old be having tantrums every day and threatening to hit her younger brother?' I nod with empathy and express how hard it can be for us to witness our kids in pain. I ask them both how they feel when Hannah gets upset.*
>
> *John shares that for the first five years, Hannah was so 'good'. 'She always did what we asked and never got upset, but since she started school, there have been explosions every day. I just don't want her to feel upset, so I try to fix whatever is happening. But it just doesn't seem to work anymore.'*
>
> *Sarah shares how when she sees Hannah start expressing big feelings, she wants to start crying herself. 'I don't know what is wrong with me, but I just panic and want it to stop.'*
>
> *I explain to Sarah and John that there is nothing wrong with Hannah or them and that Hannah is simply trying to express feelings to heal from her experiences. Being six years old can be hard; school can be challenging; having a younger sibling can be painful, and powerlessness is common at that age. 'Her expressing in this way is actually really healthy,' I say.*
>
> *Sarah sighs and says, 'But I feel so upset when she does. I just want her*

> to be happy.' I dig a little deeper and ask Sarah and John if they can remember what happened to them when they were younger. 'How did your parents respond when you were upset?' I ask.
>
> Sarah starts to cry and shares that whenever she got upset as a child, she was locked in the pantry. She was told that she could come out when she had 'stopped being silly'. Crying wasn't tolerated. She says that sometimes she wet herself because she felt so scared.
>
> John says that when someone got upset in his house, there was a 'no-fuss' response and whatever the issue, it got fixed immediately. 'There is always a solution,' his dad said, 'Smile on your dial, mate. Don't be upset!' John continued, 'They never said, "don't cry", but we just knew that our tears weren't welcome.'

Sarah and John's stories are similar to many we have heard. Well-meaning, concerned parents wanting to raise healthy and happy children, yet the effects of their own upbringings and conditioning surface and deeply affect their parenting. Hannah's feelings were helping them tap into their childhood imprints that the expression of feelings was not welcome. Thirty years later, those hurts were bubbling up when their daughter cried. Sarah and John's example shows how the past is often having a profound impact on the present, and particularly on our own thoughts, feelings and responses to our children.

While we advocate our inner reparenting and exploring the impact of our own childhoods on our outer parenting (and will talk about this later in the book), the effects of the past often extend from before our own childhoods. Parenting is part of a lineage. Trauma gets passed down from generation to generation if not attended to. However, it's not only our own particular heritage that shapes us. The culture that we've been brought up in has a profound effect on our core beliefs about the true nature of human beings, which of course, affect our parenting.

At this bigger picture level, the core paradigm for many hundreds of years in industrialised countries has been what Marion calls the 'Disconnected Domination Culture' (DDC), which is based on two things: disconnection and power-over. Disconnection shows up in the often-seen physical and emotional separation of babies and children from parents and the ways in which parents are encouraged for their baby or child to be 'independent' as soon as possible. Power-over includes punishment, threats and coercion of children and the belief that parents are designed to make children do what parents want. This profound disconnection and power-over has been passed down from generation to generation.

In more recent years, each new generation has had increasingly more compassionate and conscious ways of perceiving and treating children, which has radiated out into relationships between adults too. Yet, the most common parenting practices in industrialised nations is still based on that Disconnected Domination paradigm. The core belief is that human beings are essentially 'bad' and need to be taught, through punishment, rewards, shame and teaching, to be 'good'.

In the 1950s, behaviourism and behaviour modification techniques emerged as the new wave in psychology. As the name says, behaviourism was all about behaviour. Based on experiments with rats and dogs, practices like time-out were developed to change behaviour. Despite being formulated over seventy years ago, behaviour modification techniques are still alive today. But behaviour modification only sees behaviour. It doesn't see children as sentient beings with feelings and needs. It doesn't address WHY a child behaves the way they do, so it never addresses the true origin of behaviour. In Chapter 2, we'll explore authoritarian parenting, closely linked to behaviourism and the Disconnected Domination paradigm, and we will contrast it to Aware Parenting.

In the 1960s, a new wave of consciousness emerged, where feelings, freedom and autonomy were welcomed. Along with that, in psychology, people such as Carl Rogers and paradigms such as humanistic psychology brought in the concepts of empathy and listening to feelings. This coincided with a new era of parenting, where the attachment needs of babies and children were valued, and where natural birth and co-sleeping re-entered industrialised countries.

And then, in the 1980s, Aware Parenting came along. Aware Parenting is based on three core aspects: the first of those is attachment-style parenting, which had already been re-emerging in cultures which had lost connection with it, often centuries before. This is a returning to traditional practices of keeping babies and children close and adding to that new findings in pre- and peri-natal psychology which showed the importance of responding promptly and accurately to the needs of babies and children.

The second aspect of Aware Parenting, non-punitive discipline, is based on a fundamentally different paradigm to behaviour modification, because rather than punishments or rewards, it is all about looking underneath behaviour to its root cause. Rather than harsh beliefs that a human's true nature is 'bad', Aware Parenting holds that we are inherently aware and cooperative. Instead of punishing and rewarding children to 'make' them cooperative and calm, Aware Parenting addresses what is getting in the way of children naturally being the compassionate and cooperative beings they can be so that parents don't ever need to turn to punishments and rewards.

The third aspect is the understanding of the vulnerability of babies and children, and how they are affected by stress, mini-traumas and larger traumas. They are deeply affected by their birth and early childhood. However, alongside this is the knowledge that babies are born with inbuilt processes to heal from stress and trauma through crying, raging, laughter and play with the loving support of a parent. This third principle is often one that differs most from other parenting paradigms.

## The evolution of consciousness is reflected in an evolution in parenting approaches

With Aware Parenting, we can help children return to their true cooperative and calm nature, which is very different to 'making' them behave in the ways we want them to because they're scared of what will happen if they don't. Aware Parenting also helps us understand why children who have been brought up with attachment style principles but without an understanding of the effects of, and healing from, stress and trauma can sometimes end up waking up a lot at night, hitting, or being 'whiny' or 'clingy'.

But parenting isn't just about day-to-day behaviour. It has a powerful effect on the long-term emotional wellbeing of young people. We need only look around us today to see the devastating effects of Disconnected Domination Culture parenting paradigms. Rising rates of addiction, depression and suicide show us the profoundly painful personal impact of disconnection, shaming, punishment, and distraction from feelings. The core elements of Aware Parenting offer the exact opposite – connection, non-punitive discipline and healing through the healthy expression of feelings.

When parents share about what they want for their children, they often talk about resilience and the capacity to face life's difficulties. Older parenting paradigms have championed being 'robust' and 'tough' without understanding how important the expression of feelings is for true emotional wellbeing. In our combined decades of working with parents, we see again and again how different things can be when these Aware Parenting principles are put into practice. Through connection, compassionate understanding and listening to feelings, parents can raise children who feel deeply and compassionately connected with themselves and others.

When we understand the bigger picture and history of parenting, we can more easily feel compassion for ourselves. Have you found that as you have been reading? Of course it can sometimes be so hard to respond in these new ways, given what we have experienced. It's normal that our default response

– especially if we're stressed or stretched – is to revert to those old-fashioned ways of thinking and responding.

At this bigger picture level, Aware Parenting isn't just about helping raise connected, compassionate, and truly resilient beings or even helping us heal from our own childhoods. It's literally about evolution in consciousness. Changing how we think about and respond to children affects what they believe about themselves, how they feel, and how they behave, and this has a profound impact on the culture and the world. We see this every day in the parents we work with. More connection between parents and children. More relaxed, calm and compassionate families. More harmony. Less aggression and power-over. Qualities that are all so desperately needed in our world today.

So as you read this book, you're not only increasing your understanding of your child/ren and yourself; you're also part of bringing a new consciousness into the world. We thank you!

**CHAPTER 2**

# Feelings and Behaviour

*'You can't control me!' Sakura yells as she slams her fist down on the kitchen table. Her dad responds loudly: 'We are in charge, and as long as you live under this roof, you will do as we say.'*

*Sakura walks off and slams her door. She is seething, full of feelings of powerlessness and the pain of not being heard and yelled at by her father. She knows she lied to her parents, but she had no choice. She really wanted to go and meet those boys with her best friend. They had been planning it for ages, and she knew her parents would never let her. So she had to find another way.*

*Two days earlier, she'd asked her mum, 'Is it okay if I go to Midori's place after school to finish our assignment and then we'll practise shooting hoops in her backyard? Midori's mum can drop me home after we have dinner.'*

*'Okay, as long as you get your assignment done and don't spend the whole time chatting,' said her mum.*

*There is a little buzz awakening in Sakura; she is excited by the plan to meet the boys. She knows she lied but saw it as her only option. Sakura understands that her parents don't want her 'wasting her time' as they see it. They believe that she should be either studying, playing sports or practising piano. They have very high expectations of her to do well. They are both high achievers, so she knows it probably won't fly if she asks to meet her friend after school. For Sakura, this year is a big year. It's about forming relationships and belonging, which is so important to her, as is so natural for teens. So she told her parents what they wanted to hear.*

*However, as Sakura's mum is driving home from the supermarket, she sees some kids crossing the road, laughing and chatting. The girls look dressed up and vaguely familiar, and then she realises that one of them is her daughter. She is filled with a sense of dread as she realises her daughter isn't where she said she would be.*

*When she gets home, she's confused and angry and shares with Sakura's Dad what she'd seen. They text their daughter to see if she'll tell them the truth. They ask how the studying is going. Sakura instantly replies: 'It's going great: we've nearly finished our assignment.' Both parents feel a sense of rage as they see their daughter lying to them in front of their eyes.*

*When Sakura is dropped home, they confront her, and she comes clean. She says she just wanted to hang out with her new friends. They express their disapproval of her lying and explain that there will be consequences. She is grounded for two weeks, and they will take her phone from her every night at 6 p.m. for a month, to teach her a lesson.*

*So what can Sakura do? She feels angry, hurt, and most of all, deeply disconnected from her parents. Her overwhelming thoughts are that they don't understand her and are trying to control her life. How on earth will she survive without her phone in the evenings? That is when everyone is talking. This is her lifeline.*

*She has an idea. There's an old phone of her brother's in the cupboard, and her mum is so clueless about technology; so she puts a pic of her and her friends as a screen saver on the old phone, and at 6 p.m. the following evening, she walks into the kitchen and hands over the old phone. 'Here you go, Mum. I know these are the rules.'*

*She is praised for being 'good', but inside she is torn. One part gets some acknowledgement by being the 'good girl', and the other feels shame when she thinks about the lie she is creating. She believes what her parents have told her, that she is being 'bad' in deliberately trying to deceive them. But she feels powerless and is doing this out of desperation to get her needs met.*

*At night, she is on her phone and messages friends until late. She starts experimenting with taking pictures of herself in provocative poses. She figures that since she is lying anyway, she may as well keep going. She likes the attention she's getting, which she's certainly not getting from her parents. She realises that if she can lie about this, she can lie about many things. Play the game. Her parents will be none the wiser. They think they are getting what they want – a 'good girl'.*

You may read this story and feel angry seeing that Sakura lied. You may judge that she 'should' tell the truth and that she 'deserves' the consequences of her actions. Or you may feel judgement towards Sakura's parents for being 'controlling' and too harsh.

From an Aware Parenting perspective, what we see here is disconnection and a lack of understanding. Parents who feel scared and worried when they think about their daughter's future, and in wanting the best for her, place high expectations on her, just as they do on themselves. We also see a thirteen-year-old who wants to spread her wings, and learn about who she is, but doesn't think that she will receive love or support if she does.

Punishing our children for doing things we don't want them to do never brings the effects we desire. It creates disconnection in the relationship and forces children to look for other ways to get their needs met: through lying, hiding behaviours or completely rejecting us as parents and turning to their peers for the connection they crave. In *Hold on to Your Kids*, Gordon Neufeld and Gabor Maté highlighted the devastating impacts when teens focus all their attachment needs on their peers because they are not getting that from their parent/s.

The behaviour modification paradigm says that if we want a child or teen to behave in the ways we want them to, we need to do things to them that they find painful, seen in phrases such as 'they need to be taught a lesson'. The behaviour modification belief is that they need to be punished and then they will learn never to do it again. But this only usually 'works' if the child experiences that their relationship with the parent is in jeopardy, so they must 'do what they're told' to be loved. Their behaviour then stems from a need for secure attachment and love rather than from a true desire to cooperate and contribute.

If reading this, you were judging the parents or Sakura, we invite you to remember that harsh judgement is all part of that Disconnected Domination Culture we talked about. Instead of judgement, we can look with compassionate curiosity – not only towards Sakura, but also for her parents.

*Sakura's parents turned to punishment, and we can see that they were doing that from their own feelings of fear and powerlessness as well as their lack of trust in their daughter. If we believe that our child/ren's true nature (and our own) is inherently bad, how can we possibly trust them (or ourselves)?*

Growing up in this paradigm, most of us came to believe that punishment was 'for our own good,' that there was something inherently 'wrong' or 'bad' about us, that we 'deserved' to be shamed, and that the painful things that our parents did were our fault. Our ancestors have been conditioned for hundreds if not thousands of years to believe that we are inherently 'bad' and can't be trusted, and it is common that we automatically pass these beliefs on to our children.

Humans have evolved beyond these old-fashioned beliefs in many other areas. Aware Parenting brings a deep understanding of the true nature of human beings and the innate wisdom of our bodies into the parenting realm. We are not 'bad' or wrong beings who need to be taught to be 'good'. No! We are wired for connection and healing, and given an environment that understands and supports that, we are loving, we want to cooperate and contribute, without ever needing to be rewarded for doing so or punished for not. Painful or challenging behaviour always has a reason, whether we are a child, teen or adult, and Aware Parenting has the code for not only understanding that source, but also the solution for how to respond to it in both effective and empathic ways.

This is what we're here to help you with – finding deep compassionate understanding not only for your child/ren but also for yourself and others. Regaining that deep trust in your child's true nature and your own – and replacing the old, harsh and punitive conditioning with a deep trust in human beings' inherent awareness and lovingness – which makes tangible differences in how you relate to yourself and your child/ren.

## Parenting Paradigms

In the previous chapter, we invited you to see the bigger picture and the past so that you could see the present more clearly. In this chapter, we invite you to understand the three types of parenting more clearly. These paradigms lie on a spectrum, which we may move along at different times, depending on the stresses we experience, the age of our child, and other factors.

On one side of the spectrum is the authoritarian paradigm. Parents have power-over children, teaching them what they believe is 'right' and 'wrong' and making them behave in helpful ways. This style of parenting values the parent's perspective rather than the child's. Techniques include power-over, punishment, coercion, threat, harshness, and in the violent version, physical force and corporal punishment. Effects for children include lying, rebellion, submission, fear or compliance. There is an underlying disconnection because the parents aren't truly seeing or understanding the child's needs, feelings and perspective.

Rewards might be used to entice the child to do what the parent wants. We often see a lack of intrinsic motivation in children who are promised rewards for doing what others want them to do. In other words, a child acts in the way a parent wants, but not because they feel an inner call to do so, rather, because they want the reward that their action will lead to.

Children growing up with this parenting style can become authoritarian themselves. The powerlessness they felt was so painful that they used power-over to try to regain their sense of power. Most adults who display signs of violence are often powerless children trying to regain a sense of control in their lives in unhealthy ways.

The other outcome of authoritarian parenting is a child falling into the archetype of the 'good girl' or 'good boy' who believes that to be loved, they must behave in ways others deem acceptable. They can become adults who frequently worry about what others think and are afraid to take risks and step out of their comfort zone for fear of ridicule or judgement, with an internal dialogue full of self-judgement and shame.

On the other side of the spectrum is permissive parenting, where a child's needs are apparently paramount. Permissive parenting values the child's perspective rather than the parent's. Techniques include distraction and pleading, trying to keep the child happy at all costs and a lack of limits. It's often challenging for the parent to say 'no'. The effects for parents can include powerlessness, frustration, resentment and burnout. We said 'a child's needs are apparently paramount' because when parents consistently try to fix things to get rid of a child's upset, the child doesn't have the opportunity to express feelings that actually need to be heard. Children can then often end up being agitated and antsy and can lack compassion and understanding for others because of all the accumulated feelings they haven't been able to express. This parenting style also gives the child all the power and responsibility in the relationship, which is too much for them and is not theirs, and which can have painful consequences in later life.

Many parents we have worked with who grew up in permissive families often say they longed for clear Limits and Loving Limits[1] where parents clearly expressed a 'no' and listened lovingly to their child's feelings when they either weren't willing to do something, or when the child was acting from painful feelings.

---

1. We explain Limits and Loving Limits on p.36

One mother described her upbringing in this way:

> *My mother grew up with a strict father who would yell and never listen to her side of the story, and his default line was 'Because I said so'. My mother said she never felt that she could share what she thought or felt because whatever she said was usually shut down. So when my mum became a parent, she swore we wouldn't grow up in that angry environment. But she swung too hard in the other direction. She never said no, never got involved when my brother and I fought and said yes to anything I wanted to do. I got the sense that she wanted me to be happy at all costs. At thirteen, when I was going to parties, trying alcohol and getting into all sorts of trouble with boys, she didn't say anything. I wanted her to lean in close and say: 'I don't want you doing those things right now. I'm not willing for you to go to parties. When you are a bit older, you can explore those more.' Instead, there were no limits, and I got into many sticky situations because I thought if they were challenging enough, she would come and say no to me and listen to my feelings. I was calling out for her love and for reassurance that she cared about me, and for guidance with all that I was finding hard.*

## Conditional Love

In both these styles of parenting, we see conditional love.

In authoritarian parenting, the parent is effectively saying: 'If you do what I want, I will love you.'

This leaves the child with a conditional sense of love, believing they are only loved and accepted when they act in certain ways. This means they must hide aspects of themselves, including many of their feelings, and become who their parents want them to be rather than who they really are. This can lead to a sense of not being themselves, of aimlessness, depression and self-judgement in adult years.

In permissive parenting, the parent is communicating: 'If I do what you want, you will love me.'

This often comes from a parent's own unmet needs for empathy and love as a child, which are now being transferred on to their own child. The parent might believe, 'if I meet all my child's needs and they never feel upset, then they will love me, and I will feel comfortable in myself.'

Looking at parenting through an Aware Parenting lens, we can respond compassionately to ourselves or other parents in either of these sides of the spectrum. In both cases, the parent is living from the unmet needs and painful unexpressed feelings of their own inner child. It's with this deep compassion for ourselves that we can begin to move towards a more central place of parenting.

The middle ground on this spectrum, which Aletha Solter calls 'democratic parenting', is where Aware Parenting sits. This is based on valuing and listening to the feelings, needs and preferences of both children and adults. Thus it is inherently about connection, authenticity, expression, listening and healing.

The aim here is to respond to our child/ren with love and empathy and to look behind the behaviour, knowing that a child has important and legitimate reasons for acting how they do. We can also respond in authentic ways to our child rather than some forced 'consistency' that many parenting paradigms espouse, which means saying 'no' when we don't want to do something and listening to our child's feelings in response. This is termed a 'Limit' in Aware Parenting – something that parents on the permissive side tend to find hard to do, for fear of loss of love from their child. We can also learn how to offer Loving Limits when a child is doing something caused by painful feelings, such as hitting, throwing, or doing something they know we don't want them to do, where we say no to the behaviour and yes to the underlying feelings. Loving Limits tend to be lacking in permissive parenting, because saying 'no' is hard there, and also don't happen in authoritarian parenting, where limits tend to be harsh or punitive. 'Loving Limits' is a term that Marion developed and we will talk about them in more detail later in the book.

The non-punitive element of Aware Parenting is exactly that – rather than using punishments and rewards, we support our children to want to cooperate and contribute, to be naturally gently and considerate, by helping them with whatever is getting in the way of that behaviour, using the practices and processes we talk about in this book. Aware Parenting values connection, communication and trust. Its motto is: 'How do we both get our needs met here?'

## Meeting Needs

So how could Sakura's story unfold differently through an Aware Parenting lens?

Our first response as parents in this situation could be to connect in with how we feel, listening to our feelings of anger and frustration and hear what they are telling us. Perhaps our child's behaviour reminds us of a childhood experience when we were lied to. Maybe we feel sadness as we think about the disconnect in our relationship with our child, and remember that it wasn't always this way. Our top priority is to attend to our own feelings, because the more our feelings are heard, the more we will return to our own state of calm and will be more likely to be able to respond calmly to our child/ren.

As calm adults, we can begin the conversation from a place of connection, trust and love instead of fear and anger. When we can connect with compassion for our child rather than judgement, understanding there are important reasons for their behaviour, our child is likely to experience a sense of safety, and honest communication is much more likely.

As parents, we could acknowledge that Sakura lied because she was scared about what would happen if she told the truth. Emotional safety in the relationship is the parent's responsibility. Our role is to keep creating that connection and safety so that no matter what happens, the child feels safe enough to tell us what's really going on. In taking responsibility for the child's emotional safety, we reclaim our true power as parents and we are less likely to feel powerless and to give our children responsibility for our needs and feelings.

We could also remember that our children will not always make the wisest of decisions and that these experiences – if responded to with compassionate and enquiring conversation – can lead to growth and wisdom through experience, i.e. true resilience. In contrast, if we shame or punish them, we limit their opportunity for growth and learning. The child becomes more consumed with the feelings of disconnection from their attachment source and the pain that comes from being judged and will learn to judge themselves when they do things they later regret. This has long-term effects that you might even recognise in yourself.

If we approach the situation with our child with an understanding that unwise decisions are part of learning and growing and hold in mind, 'each time you do something that isn't so wise, I will be here to listen, be your guide and help you,' we are giving the compassionate message that we are all constantly learning and they are loved unconditionally and will always have support when they need it.

Then we can open up the communication, 'I would love to hear what was going on for you, honey. I'm sorry if I didn't make it safe enough for you to tell me the truth. I would love to hear how you are feeling.' And then we can listen. Really listen. Without jumping in and giving our opinion, without judging them or shaming them, but instead supporting them to express their thoughts and feelings.

Once we have finished listening, we could share our thoughts or concerns. Perhaps one of your family values is knowing where your child is. The question then becomes, 'how could we do it differently next time so that we can both get our needs met?' What could we change or shift so we can make it safer and also honour our teen's need for autonomy and exploration?

We can see the two different outcomes from these two scenarios. In the first one, there is an increasing disconnection between Sakura and her parents and more entrenchment into painful conclusions about each other. In the second, there is reconnection and repair – the building of connection and trust and a sense of growing and healing together.

One of the fundamental pieces missing in many parenting philosophies is understanding that a child's external state is a reflection of their internal world. All behaviour is attempting to communicate something. In Lael's terminology, this is being either 'in balance' or 'out of balance'.

The concept of balance is also related to homeostasis, which is when the body is free from stress. This form of balance is different to the balance of attention, a term we talk about later in the book.

When a child is in balance, they are calm and emotionally spacious. We may hear them singing in their bedroom or snuggling the family pet. We hear them talk lovingly to their siblings, and when we ask them to pick up their shoes, they usually do it willingly. We all have experiences of our children feeling joyous, happy and content. Their bodies are relaxed, and their nervous system is calm.

When a child is out of balance, we see all the other types of behaviours, which may be agitated or dissociated. They may walk past their sister and punch her in the arm. They may say that nothing is ever how they want it to be. You may ask them to stop throwing the ball at the wall, and they look at you and keep doing it. Behaviours can also include hitting, yelling, swearing, agitation, reluctance or refusal to cooperate and whining. Or they might be withdrawn, spaced out, not listening, not responding, with eyes gazing into space or at a book or a screen. Although not as obviously out of balance, these behaviours also show a child who is stressed and has painful feelings inside.

Aware Parenting asks us to see a child out of balance as trying to communicate something. We see it as a child waving a red flag, saying, 'I have something going on for me, and I need your help with it.' If we meet this behaviour with punishment, yelling, judgement or ignoring, we're missing an opportunity to support a child to offload what is stirring inside them and for us to experience the fulfilment of supporting their natural return to balance and homeostasis. Children want to feel calm and relaxed. They want to be able to sleep when they're tired, look into our eyes, and be able to concentrate on things that they enjoy. They aren't doing these things deliberately, and they need our help when they are doing them.

*A child's natural state is to feel connected and calm, but often big feelings bubble up and get in the way.*

## What Causes a Child to be Out of Balance?

We have discussed looking behind the behaviour to discover and attend to the cause. We've also explained how being out of balance leads to our child/ren doing things we don't enjoy. But what actually leads to a child being out of balance in the first place? Let's look at that in more detail now.

There are three main causes for children being out of balance:[2]

1. What they're thinking
2. What they're needing.
3. What they're feeling.

Each of these causes profoundly affects the sensations and feelings that a child experiences. (These are all relevant for us as parents, too, as we will be sharing about in the next chapter.)

### 1. *What They're Thinking (and What They Understand)*

Our child's understanding of a situation profoundly affects their feelings and actions. This is why understanding their level of cognitive development is so important. This includes understanding their thoughts about us and why we're doing what we're doing, and also what they're thinking about themselves. Their thoughts affect how they feel in their bodies, and those feelings influence their behaviour.

---

1. Adapted by Marion from Aletha Solter's list of three causes of challenging behaviours.

For example:

- A two-year-old might not yet understand that pulling all the toilet paper off the toilet roll means it's hard to use and goes everywhere and so might go ahead and unroll all five rolls.
- A five-year-old with a new sibling might think we don't love them anymore when they see us cuddling and kissing the baby. Those thoughts might cause jealousy and grief, and those feelings might bubble up and turn into pinching the baby if not expressed through crying and raging.
- An eleven-year-old might think they're stupid when their schoolwork was given a low mark. Those harsh thoughts lead to painful feelings, perhaps leading to them not wanting to do their homework.

Responding to our children with information helps them, but only when a lack of information is the cause of the feelings. When we let our two-year-old know that we want to keep the toilet paper on the roll and give them something similar to play with, we're finding ways to meet everyone's needs. The cause of the behaviour was a lack of information, so giving information alters the behaviour.

However, when children are telling themselves painful thoughts, sometimes it's not enough to give them accurate information – such as telling our five-year-old that we still love them even though we're cuddling their sibling; or expressing to our eleven-year-old that they aren't stupid. Once their thoughts have also created feelings, we also need to address them on a feeling level, as we'll explore in #3 below.

This information/cognitive level is often addressed in other parenting paradigms, where a child might be repeatedly told, 'it hurts if you hit'. However, cognitive understanding is only one of the causes of behaviour. If we are giving information about how unbrushed teeth get cavities and our child is still not brushing their teeth, we know that it's probably not information or a lack of understanding that is the cause of the behaviour.

Having information about these three causes of behaviour can be life-changing for parents. If we believe that the child's behaviour is only caused by what they think, and they keep doing things we don't want them to do, our next conclusion will be they are doing it deliberately, they are choosing to do it, and they are enjoying it. With those thoughts, we are likely to start feeling frustrated, powerless or angry ourselves. If we add to that conditioned beliefs about inherent badness and that our only choices are teaching, coercion, reward or punishment, often power-over becomes the default.

But if we know there are three reasons, and we've tried the first reason, and we've given them information, we still have choice and agency. We have more information and understanding as parents, and we can then attend to those other two reasons (#2 needs and #3 feelings) to discover which one is the cause and, thus, what we can do to help them return to calmness. In having our own needs for understanding met, we can feel true power as parents.

## 2. What They're Needing

We know from our own experiences that unmet needs create painful feelings. Have you ever been desperate for rest or support or empathy and felt agitated and frustrated? At times like that, perhaps you don't want to cooperate with your child's request for another story; and you're more likely to respond with a harsh tone of voice and use power-over when they don't do as you ask? We can clearly see that link between our unmet needs, the agitation we feel in our bodies, and how much that affects our behaviour.

Children are just like us. When they need connection or support or empathy or autonomy, their bodies create feelings to alert them to those unmet needs. A need for connection can create sadness and loneliness, just as a need for food leads to a feeling of hunger, and a need for autonomy can be followed by a feeling of frustration. These uncomfortable feelings alert our children to do what they can to meet those needs.

Yet, those feelings feel uncomfortable, and as they accumulate, they lead to agitation in the body. This agitation shows up when they're being 'silly' in the supermarket, won't sit still at the table, or are pushing their younger sibling.

See how much we miss and misunderstand them when we tell them, 'stop being silly', 'sit still', or, 'be gentle'? They're not choosing to do those things. The child's unmet needs create agitated feelings which then lead to the behaviour.

Giving them information in these situations doesn't address the source of the behaviour, so it won't lead to a change in their behaviour. If we think that the information is what is causing the behaviour, we're likely to feel even more frustrated, or we'll move to either harshness or distraction to try to change the behaviour. Whereas, if we understand that their behaviour is caused by an unmet need, and we meet the original need, the discomfort leaves, leaving our child to return to feeling calm and able to cooperate.

## 3. What They're Feeling

We have already outlined how thoughts can lead to feelings and how unmet needs can lead to feelings and how both of these lead to children behaving in ways we find challenging. This third type of feeling which affects behaviour is caused by emotions from the present and past that were caused by stress, mini-trauma or larger trauma. It's normal and natural for every child to feel many painful feelings – however much we aim to meet their needs and respond empathically.

For example, children can feel:

- Overwhelmed at the shopping centre or family gathering.
- Confused when watching a movie designed for older children or adults.
- Powerless when another child takes something from them or when their parents argue or separate.
- Jealous when a sibling is receiving lots of attention.
- Sad when they're away from us.
- Scared if we get angry or act in unpredictable ways.
- Terror from unhealed trauma from their birth experience or from being separated after birth.

Our child/ren's feelings are just as real as ours. When those feelings don't get to be expressed and lovingly heard, they accumulate in a child's body. That accumulation leads to agitation. And when they're agitated, it's really hard for them to sleep, sit still, concentrate, think clearly, cooperate or be gentle. They have no choice over this. They're not choosing it. They're not doing it deliberately. The feelings lead to agitation, and the agitation deeply affects their behaviour.

As you read this, we wonder if it helps you understand even more clearly how the behaviour modification approach and the Disconnected Domination paradigm do a great disservice to children (and adults too).

How do you feel and what do you think when you imagine a child in the following three situations?

- A two-year-old runs in from outside, joyfully wanting to tell his dad about how much fun he's had in the garden but is shouted at for getting mud on the rug. How might he feel? What conclusions might he make about himself and his relationship with his dad?
- A five-year-old who's been away from her mother all day keeps talking whilst her mother is trying to speak on the phone and is sent to her room to be quiet. How might she feel?
- A thirteen-year-old with separated parents is constantly biting her nails, and her dad threatens to take away her pocket money if she doesn't stop. What might she believe about her dad's love for her?

Perhaps in some kind of ideal world, our two-year-old would stop running on the rug and say, 'Sorry, Daddy! I was just having so much fun I didn't realise I was spreading mud everywhere and I didn't know that you don't like mud on the rug. I will help you clean it up! Could you please tell me what you're happy for me to do and what you don't want me to do because I'm still learning about all that stuff!'

Or a five-year-old might wait patiently for half an hour and then express, 'Sorry, Mum! I'm sad. I've missed you, and I really wanted to tell you all about my day because I love talking with you. I want to be close to you and be sure that you still love me. I really need love and connection and reassurance.'

Or the thirteen-year-old would nod and acknowledge her father's threat and say, 'Thanks for reminding me, Dad. I'm feeling scared and unsure about what's happening in our home, and I am biting my nails to try to stop feeling the feelings because they are so overwhelming for me. Would you be willing to hold me in your arms whilst I cry and tell you how scared I am?'

We can see how unrealistic it is to expect the above responses from children. Even most adults don't possess the capabilities to understand the causes of their behaviour, express their needs and feelings eloquently, take responsibility for their behaviour and ask for what they really need to bring them back to a calm centre.

The more we understand these three causes (thinking/understanding, needs and feelings) for our child/ren's behaviour, the more likely we will be able to respond empathically and effectively. In any moment, that might mean giving them clear and age-appropriate information, meeting their here-and-now needs, or listening to their painful feelings. The more we can respond to their behaviours with a response which matches the cause of the behaviour, the more they will feel calm and relaxed in their bodies and their behaviour will reflect that.

The other wonderful thing is that our children give us plenty of opportunities to repair, reconnect, and apologise for all the times we didn't understand the cause of their behaviours and didn't respond in matching or helpful ways! So, even if these concepts are new, it's never too late to implement them and to repair.

## CHAPTER 3

# Understanding Children's Feelings

*There had been a big build-up to this special day. Ryder had been talking about it for weeks! Most of his kindergarten class was coming to his fifth birthday. His parents had hired a huge inflatable jumping castle, and his dad Dan was making him a Paw Patrol birthday cake. Ryder had woken up at 6.30 a.m., asking how much longer it would be until everyone came to his party.*

*As 11 a.m. rolled around, fifteen kids and their parents filled the house. There was a lot of shrieking as the kids played together. Ryder didn't know it, but soon a clown would be arriving to do magic and make balloon animals. Ryder's parents wanted this to be a gorgeous day for him. They were so happy that their lovely boy was turning five.*

*Amelia and her mum Penny arrive a little late. At kindergarten, Amelia loved playing with Ryder in the sandpit in the playground under a big tree, and they often made tunnels and tracks with the cars and trains. As soon as they arrived at the party, Amelia clung to her mum's leg. She often felt overwhelmed at parties, with all the people and noise. She also felt a little scared in strange new houses and hadn't been to Ryder's house before. Penny ushered her in the door. 'Sweetie, would you like to say hello to Ryder and give him his present?' Amelia didn't want to move from the safety of her mum's legs, but she took the present, half-threw it at Ryder and managed a little hello.*

*Axel and Ryder had been talking about this party all week. Axel was Ryder's best mate, and they regularly hung out together. Their parents often caught up for cups of tea, so they spent lots of time on the trampoline or building Lego worlds. Axel's mum, Valeria ran after him* up the driveway into Ryder's house once they got there; he was desperate to get inside and play.

The clown arrived, and Ryder was so surprised that he jumped up and down and started making funny noises. The kids thought it was hysterical. Amelia hung at the back and thought the clown was funny but didn't want to sit on the rug up close. Penny kept encouraging her forward, but she preferred to watch from afar.

The two-hour party passed quickly, and as it was beginning to wind up, Ryder asked if he could open his presents. 'Sure, Ryder,' said Dan. 'But just one or two presents; I'd like you to leave the rest for later.' The kids gathered in a circle, and Ryder ripped open the first present. It was a new Lego set, and he was excited. 'Dad,' he yelled, 'can we build this now?' Dan replied they would do it after the party.

Axel is eyeing the Lego. He really wants this set. He's been asking his mum for it for ages. He starts edging closer to the box. Ryder thanks his friend for the Lego and reaches for another present. This time it's a drawing set. He doesn't like drawing that much; he much prefers building stuff. He lets out a sigh, feeling a bit disappointed to receive the latest gift. 'I'm going to open another one!' he declares.

Dan, watching this play out, jumps in. 'Hey, Ryder! I only want you to open those two presents for now; I'd like you to leave the rest until later because the party is ending, and I'd love you to have time to say goodbye to your friends.'

Ryder looks at his dad and starts crying; 'No! I want to open more! I don't like the drawing set; I want other ones. I want to open more, *NOW!*'

Dan thinks, 'Oh, maybe he can open another one. It's not a big deal. He did say two, but it's Ryder's birthday, and the party isn't quite finished yet. Perhaps his son can open them all.' He hears Ryder's cries getting louder and louder. Other parents are looking at him, and he starts to feel the pressure rising. 'Far out!' Dan thinks in his mind, 'I have given you everything today and more; why can't you just be grateful!' He's increasingly tense and stressed, but he remembers his love for his son and how he wants this day to be enjoyable. He takes a deep breath and gets down low to Ryder's level. 'Oh Ryder, I really understand that you want to open another present. I'm not willing for you to open any more now, but I'd love to hear you tell me how you're feeling!' Ryder falls into his dad's arms, lets out a big wail of emotions, and the overwhelm of the day starts to be released.

As all this unfolds, Axel picks up the Lego and takes it into the corner. He wants to open it. Valeria sees this and moves in close before he can open it. 'Axel, that isn't your present; I want you to give that back to Ryder.'

Axel pulls it closer to his chest, 'But I told you I want this one. Ryder will let me play with it!' Valeria reaches out her hand to prevent him from opening the box, and Axel hits her. 'No! I want it!'

For a moment, Valeria wants to yell back, 'That's it! You're not taking any cake or party bags home!' but she manages to stop herself. She tries to plead with him. 'Okay, sweetie, why don't we go to the toy shop on the way home and get you one?'

For a second, Axel listens as he contemplates this offer, but he has the Lego in front of him and wants to open it NOW. Valeria takes a deep breath and moves in closer; she looks Axel in the eye; 'I know you want it, honey, but it's not yours. I'm going to help you give it back to Ryder.' She picks up Axel as he starts flailing about and takes him into the other room to listen to his feelings. After letting those big feelings out, he feels naturally calmer again and is willing to give the Lego back.

*As all the tensions are coming out at the party, Amelia goes to the corner of another room. She sits huddled up, sucks her thumb and stares off into the distance. When Penny finds her, she asks, 'What are you doing here? Come and join the party!' Amelia doesn't say anything; she keeps sucking her thumb. Penny starts to feel powerless. 'Amelia, if you return to the party, we can take some cake home for Dad. He loves it when you do that!'*

*Amelia shifts her body so that her back is now towards her mother. Penny feels frustrated and even more powerless; 'Amelia, I've had enough of this. If you don't go back in now, we'll have to leave!' Amelia doesn't move, and feeling despair, Penny takes a big breath and sighs. She remembers how she felt at parties when she was five and how overwhelmed she sometimes felt. Her compassion returns. 'Being at a party with lots of people can be a lot, can't it? Are you feeling overwhelmed, sweetie?' Amelia nods and turns to her Mum.*

*Penny leans in close and whispers to her daughter, 'That thumb looks yummy. Can I have some?' Amelia's eyes sparkle a little, and Penny senses a window of connection. 'Hmm, I'd like some, please!' Amelia giggles. They play for a minute, giggling and pretending to munch on thumbs and fingers. Penny softens, and so does Amelia. 'Honey, I see you feel overwhelmed with everyone here. Would you like for us to find a comfy corner in the party room, and you can sit on my lap, and we just watch?' Amelia nods and takes her mum's hand, and they rejoin the party as the goodbyes start to happen.*

## Understanding Children's Feelings

In the last chapter, we discussed the three causes of behaviour: thinking/understanding, needs and feelings. In this chapter, we are narrowing our focus to children's feelings. As we previously shared, however much we aim to respond promptly and accurately to our child/ren's needs, they all will experience uncomfortable feelings at times. The full range of feelings often comes from them experiencing not-enough or too-much. The not-enough comes from unmet needs such as holding, closeness, understanding, touch, presence, and attunement to their needs. The too-much comes with experiences that are frightening, overwhelming or painful, where things happen to them that they don't want to happen, or where their 'no' isn't heard. We can categorise these as stresses, mini-traumas or larger traumas.

In response to these situations, they feel feelings such as:

- discomfort
- confusion
- overwhelm
- frustration
- helplessness
- powerlessness
- sadness
- fear
- terror
- rage
- shock

And of course, they experience the full range of feelings that come from met needs (enough-ness) and enjoyable experiences (that aren't too much), as well as their own innate state, such as:

- curiosity
- wonder
- happiness
- delight
- joy
- excitement

## What Causes These Feelings?

As you read this, we invite you to be compassionate with yourself and any feelings you might feel. The particular situations where the child might feel uncomfortable or painful feelings are:

- In the womb, where they might feel fear, discomfort, or stress.
- During birth, where they could feel overwhelm, fear, terror, rage, helplessness, or powerlessness.
- If separated after birth, they might feel confusion, sadness, loss, fear, terror, rage, or helplessness.
- If they experience medical procedures during or after birth or in childhood, including dental visits, they could experience pain, helplessness, frustration, fear, terror, or rage.
- If left alone to cry, they might feel scared, overwhelmed, confused, terrified, or helpless.
- Going out to shops or busy places, they could experience confusion, overwhelm, or fear.
- Loud noises could lead to emotions of confusion or shock.

- Their needs being misunderstood could lead to confusion, sadness or helplessness.
- Being left alone could bring feelings of fear, loss, sadness, confusion, or helplessness.
- Parents' feelings of confusion, fear, or sadness can be passed onto their child/ren.
- Arguments could stimulate fear, shock, or confusion.
- Being pushed or treated roughly by older siblings might lead to feelings of shock, fear, or helplessness.
- With big trips, holidays, travel, or moving house, they might feel overwhelmed or confused.
- During illness, teething or accidents, they might feel confusion, shock, or overwhelm.
- During developmental leaps, they could feel frustration.
- They might feel jealous, powerless, hurt, sad, or lonely when a new sibling is born.
- They could experience being scared, afraid, helpless, or overwhelmed when they go to daycare, preschool, kindergarten or school.
- They might feel powerlessness, rage, hurt, or confusion when other children take things, hit them, or call them names.
- They could feel powerlessness, rage, confusion, loss, sadness, or hurt if their parents separate or a family member dies.

We want to remind you again if your baby or child has experienced any of these, and you think that they haven't had the chance to express those feelings yet, that it is NEVER TOO LATE. That is another wonderful thing about Aware Parenting!

Every baby, child and teen will feel different amounts of painful feelings and experience different stress levels, mini-traumas or larger traumas. In addition, babies, children and teens have different sensitivity levels. Some are more highly sensitive and will feel things more deeply and have bigger feelings after an experience than another child who isn't as sensitive. Each child is different, has a different physiology and central nervous system and will experience things in different ways. That is why, with Aware Parenting, we will keep on inviting you to observe your child. If a child is experiencing something as stressful or traumatic or is feeling overwhelmed in a situation, our first step as parents is always to do what we can to stop the stressful experience, whether that is removing them from the situation or taking away the source of the stress.

Once we understand why children have big feelings, we can see what they learn to do with these feelings. In Chapter 1, we talked about the three key types of parenting – authoritarian, permissive and democratic (Aware Parenting.) There are also three main ways that children can be with their feelings, which parallel the three types of parenting. Those are expression, suppression (and dissociation) and aggression (and agitation). Each of these three ways of being with feelings has a parallel in each of the forms of parenting:

1. Expression has parallels with democratic parenting. The parent tends to express their feelings in healthy ways and is able to support their child to express their feelings through crying, raging, laughter and play.
2. Suppression/dissociation has parallels with permissive parenting. The parent tends to dissociate from or suppress their needs and feelings and can be afraid of their own anger.
3. Aggression/agitation has parallels with authoritarian parenting. The parent tends to be in fight mode, using power-over, loudness or harshness.

Returning to the birthday story, we can see how as parents, our first go-to can often be 'permissiveness', trying to plead with our children, giving them subtle or not so subtle rewards, or distracting them from what's really going on with them and the feelings that are bubbling inside. You might have noticed that happening when Dan was tempted to say yes to Ryder opening more presents, when Valeria said she'd buy Lego for Axel and when Amelia's mum offered her cake to encourage her to come out and engage. (And at times, those might be apt responses. But in these three cases, where upset feelings from past stress and trauma rather than unmet needs were driving the three children's behaviours, trying to meet needs simply distracted them from the true feeling cause.)

When these attempts don't seem to work, and our child is still doing what we don't want them to do, powerlessness can tip us over into more authoritarian and power-over practices. That showed up in Dan's thoughts that Ryder was being ungrateful and his temptation to shame him, when Valeria was tempted to punish Axel by not taking any cake home, and when Penny threatened Amelia that if she didn't come out, they were going home.

In these three examples, the parents then chose to connect with their child and listen to the feelings causing the behaviours.

Perhaps you felt touched when you imagined Dan giving compassion to his son and opening his arms for Ryder to let out the big feelings of his big day. Or when you saw Valeria offer a Loving Limit and then listen to Axel's feelings so he could naturally return to his consideration for his friend. Or when you thought of Penny giving loving support, playing and listening to Amelia so she could feel connected and relaxed enough be a part of the party again. As explained in Chapter 2, children naturally want to return to a calm presence and are born with inbuilt processes to do that. But, because of our cultural conditioning, we may not always see, understand or welcome those ways.

## The Three Different Ways of Responding to Uncomfortable Feelings

As parents, we can observe the three ways that children react to uncomfortable feelings in their bodies – suppression, aggression and expression.

- **Suppression (and dissociation):** Commonly seen in behaviours such as thumb sucking, dummy or pacifier use, wanting to eat or watch a screen when upset, clutching onto a soft toy or a blanket, hair twirling, nose-picking and nail-biting. These are all ways that help children mildly dissociate from their feelings. (In Part II, we have a whole chapter on suppression and dissociation, and in Part III, we'll invite you to look at how you commonly suppress your feelings or dissociate from them!)

- **Aggression (and agitation):** Generally seen in behaviours such as throwing, taking, pinching, pulling, hitting, head butting and swearing, as well as hyperactivity, distractibility and 'defiance'.
- **Expression:** Commonly seen in behaviours such as crying, tantrums, laughter, play, sweating, shaking, yawning and talking.

Our natural inbuilt process as children is to return to homeostasis through this third response – expression, which generally consists of crying and raging along with vigorous movement. Due to our cultural conditioning and own childhood hurts, as parents we don't always understand this or have the emotional spaciousness to be with these natural expressions of feelings. Children need an adult to be connected and lovingly present with them to be able to express their painful feelings in these healthy ways. If we don't understand that they're trying to express feelings, or we distract them, make judgements about that expression, or we're not able to be with those same uncomfortable feelings in ourselves, or we simply can't listen because we're tired or busy or attending to another child, then those feelings don't get expressed.

Lael sometimes refers to an adult listening to big feelings as 'holding space'. This is when we are feeling calm and centred and we create a safe space for a child (or adult) to share their feelings and thoughts. This often involves being present, listening and trusting what is being expressed. It doesn't involve fixing or trying to make things better or jumping in with our own story of relating to how they feel. Holding space is simply being present with someone's upset feelings and offering them loving empathy and compassion.

## Accumulation

Because feelings are real physiological things in the body, if a child doesn't express those feelings, they accumulate in their bodies. Feelings have hormonal correlates and are related to the fight/flight response.

The fight/flight/freeze response is the body's way of protecting itself from a perceived threat. The fight response is when we respond to a perceived threat with a sense of fight, which may involve yelling or screaming or lashing out physically with our arms or legs. A flight response instructs our body to run from danger and pushes us to run away or urgently get out of a room. The freeze response is when our body becomes immobile, and it will often shut down and we will not be able to speak or take action against a threat.

Other paradigms also include the fawn response, which is a term coined by psychotherapist Pete Walker. It is when we try to please someone to avoid conflict and can often turn up in 'good girl/good boy' behaviour. This is a behavioural strategy rather than a distinct psychological state as the others are, and it is not a part of Aware Parenting terminology.

All of these responses are designed to keep us safe or survive in situations we experience as threatening. We can see that dissociation we talked about above matches the freeze response, whereas aggression and agitation, also understood as hyperarousal in Aware Parenting, match the fight/ flight response.

When a child doesn't complete the fight or flight response, the tension mobilised in their muscles to fight or flee doesn't get to be expressed or released. Those unexpressed feelings, stress hormones, and unreleased tension build up in their bodies. When feelings aren't expressed, they accumulate and lead to agitation, which can show up as:

- whining
- other agitated vocalisations
- avoiding connection
- avoiding eye contact
- not being able to concentrate
- not being able to listen
- tension in the hands and the rest of the body

- moving from one activity to the next very quickly
- constant movement
- holding in wee and poo/controlling toileting
- taking a long time to go to sleep (because it's hard to sleep when agitated)
- wriggling around whilst sleeping
- frequent night waking
- waking up easily or early before having enough sleep (because it's hard to sleep soundly when there are a whole lot of feelings inside)

Whatever percentage of feelings we don't listen to, children will then suppress, and these feelings accumulate in the child's body. Those feelings are physiological, including the muscle tension that occurs when a child hasn't been able to fully move through the fight/flight response, so they lead to a whole host of symptoms as seen above, which tend to be the things that parents commonly find challenging.

The important things to remember are:

- Babies and children aren't doing this on purpose.
- Babies and children would much prefer to feel comfortable, present and calm.
- Babies and children want to sleep when they're tired.
- Babies and children have learnt how to respond to their feelings from us.
- Babies and children need our help to be able to express their feelings.
- It's our loving presence, available attention and physical closeness which helps them experience emotional safety where their feelings are welcome so they can express those accumulated feelings.

## More About Suppression and Dissociation

If a child doesn't have the support of a loving adult listener who understands that all children have feelings to express and who is able to be with those feelings, they will generally suppress their feelings or dissociate. When they are dissociating from their feelings, they also feel more disconnected or detached from themselves and others.

We can see this clearly in Amelia's behaviour. Penny had a really painful childhood, with a dad who regularly punished her and sent her to her room. So whenever Amelia tries to express her feelings through crying, Penny feels scared and overwhelmed. She starts to panic and tries to do anything to stop Amelia from crying. Amelia has experienced Penny's fear and distraction many times, and received the message that it wasn't safe to cry, so rather than crying, she sucks her thumb whenever she needs to cry.

As well as thumb sucking, we might also see suppression or mild dissociation in the following forms:

- nail biting
- hair twirling
- nose picking
- clutching on to a soft toy or blanket
- muscle tension
- dummy use

## More About Aggression and Agitation

There's also that third way children can be with painful feelings – aggression and agitation – and we can see this in Axel. Axel's parents have recently split up. It's really natural at times like this for children to have a lot of big feelings, including powerlessness, grief and fear. Valeria and her ex have been so full up with their feelings that they haven't had much emotional bandwidth to be with Axel's feelings. Those unexpressed feelings are showing up in his hitting, which we can also think of in relation to the incomplete fight/flight response. When Valeria offers a Loving Limit (which we'll explore later in the book in more depth), the unexpressed feelings that are causing the hitting can come out and be expressed in healthy ways.

Usual forms of aggression and agitation are things like:

- pinching
- biting
- hitting
- pushing
- taking
- kicking
- hyperactivity
- agitation
- an inability to sit still
- reactivity

## More About Expression

Children will keep on trying to feel, express and release the painful feelings through things like:

- Crying or raging over small things (inviting us to lovingly listen).
- Laughter and being 'silly' (inviting us to join in with attachment play[3]).
- Doing things they know we don't want them to do (inviting us to offer a Loving Limit and listen to their feelings).

3. We will explain attachment play later in this chapter.

## Accumulated Feelings

### *Responding to Children's Painful Feelings:*

To summarise, there are three types of parenting: authoritarian, permissive and democratic. There are three reasons for unenjoyable behaviour: thoughts, needs and feelings. And there are also three[4] key ways that we can respond to children's painful feelings so that they can return to balance: connection and listening, attachment play and Loving Limits with listening to feelings. We can see these at work at Ryder's party:

- Connection and listening: This is how Dan helped Ryder, by simply listening to the feelings that were naturally bubbling up in him after a fun day that was also overwhelming, so that he'd feel calm enough to sleep that night.
- Attachment play: This is how Penny helped Amelia release some of the fear she was suppressing through thumb-sucking, so she could move into connection again.
- Loving Limits and listening to feelings: This is how Valeria said a loving 'no' to Axel's behaviour and a compassionate 'yes' to his underlying feelings of powerlessness, so that he could return to feeling calm and care for his friend again.

## Connection and Listening

In our Disconnected Domination Culture, true connection and listening are quite rare. You probably know how you feel when you're trying to share something painful, and your listener says, 'It will all pass,' 'I had something like that happen to me,' or, 'Would you like a glass of wine?'

Responding to children's painful feelings, adults may say: 'There's no need to cry,' 'Don't cry,' 'Boys don't cry,' 'There's nothing to cry about,' or 'shhh … have some chocolate.' A parent may also make fun of a child's feelings or even mock them if they think that the child's response is not warranted in certain situations.

---

[4]. You can see by now that Marion loves lists of three!

In contrast, with connection and listening, we offer our physical and emotional presence to listen to what our child is expressing. That may include using a warm tone of voice, moving closer, and offering empathy and loving support. We might say phrases such as: 'I'm here with you,' 'I see that you're upset,' 'I'm listening,' 'I won't leave you alone whilst you're upset,' 'I'm here to listen to all you want to tell me,' 'I love you'.

Connection and listening facilitate and support a child's natural expression of feelings. They are born with this natural capacity to heal from stress and trauma, to release the stress hormones and physical tension from the fight/flight response, and to feel naturally calm. Listening in this way helps them express their feelings through crying and tantrums, helps them feel safe and loved while expressing their feelings, and helps them come out the other side feeling relieved and relaxed so that they can naturally concentrate, cooperate, be gentle, and sleep peacefully.

As a culture, we often have a very conflicted relationship with tears and expressing feelings. In the Disconnected Domination paradigm, expressing tears has been seen as a sign of weakness.

For children, it's not just the expression of tears that is healing. They need to be in an adult's loving presence for healing to happen. When we talk about the healing power of crying and raging, we are always referring to that being with the loving support of an adult.

Children will save their big feelings for parents or caregivers when they have been separated for the day, such as if they've been with grandparents. Children know when they are with adults who welcome feelings and when it's safe to express their feelings and when it is not. This is why we often see children have big crying or raging episodes after kindergarten and school. Many children hold in their feelings, sensing there isn't the emotional safety for them to be heard, so they wait till they get home and then release the feelings from the stresses and mini-traumas they have experienced during the day.

On the other hand, children may at times want to do something but feel scared to do it. We can help them to develop true resilience by supporting them in letting out all the feelings related to this experience before they go to do that thing. When we create a safe space for a child to cry or share about how difficult they find that situation, the feelings are released, and with little or no fear remaining, they may then be able to move forward to do that thing that they were too scared to do before. Play can also be really helpful to release fear, and we're going to be talking about that more later too!

As an adult, you may recall times when you have felt scared, stuck or worried and expressed your thoughts, shared your fears and perhaps had a cry with someone with whom you felt safe. Afterwards, you may have felt lighter with a sense of optimism about moving forward to do the thing you wanted to do. Children are just like us in that regard.

*Our ability to express our feelings safely with another compassionate person creates true resilience that supports us to move through some of the most challenging situations that life has to offer instead of staying stuck in past trauma that can keep us scared and shut down.*

## What Happens as Children Grow?

One of the biggest concerns parents often share about listening to children's feelings is whether they will grow up to be teenagers or adults who have big meltdowns or get upset or angry all the time. From our personal experience with our own children and also the thousands of parents we have supported over the years, we see the opposite to be true.

When we hold space for children's feelings from a young age, their connection with their body and central nervous system in particular is highly attuned to when they are out of balance. When they learn from early childhood that their feelings are welcomed and there are healthy ways to express them, they have a visceral understanding of how much more comfortable they feel once they have expressed their feelings.

Lael remembers a time with her daughter when she was five: 'My daughter had some big feelings she needed to express. I didn't have the spaciousness to hold space for her feelings and I offered her some chocolate instead (as a way of suppressing her feelings or trying to distract her – all of us at certain times won't have any space to listen.) My daughter looked me in the eye and said … 'I don't want chocolate, I want you to listen to my feelings!' As a five-year-old, she knew that being able to express her feelings and being heard would help her feel way more comfortable and relaxed in her body than any chocolate could.

We have seen this so many times over the years, that when children's feelings are lovingly accepted, they often don't then get to the point of big outburst in the supermarket or being harsh or hitting to try and express the feelings that are held inside. Often they will just ask for what they need or simply share their feelings. Many parents have told us over the years about how amazed they felt, seeing their children's emotional awareness. Children of all ages can say, 'I feel angry, can you help me with my feelings,' or, 'I feel sad and need to have a cry with you.'

When feelings are welcomed and supported, a belief system is created that feelings are deeply accepted. This leads to profound compassion for others and their feelings as well as self-compassion for the wide array of emotions that we feel.

We have also observed over the years that children who are supported with their feelings grow up to be teens and young adults who don't have to look for limits to push up against to try and move big stuck feelings, nor do they need to act in ways that are harsh to others. They simply feel willing to share what is happening for them and ask for empathy, or lean into self-care practices that nourish themselves. In addition, because they have already healed from lots of stress and trauma, they have fewer accumulated feelings, so they generally feel calm and relaxed and are less likely to be reactive.

## Attachment Play

Have you ever noticed how relaxed you feel after watching a comedy on Netflix? Play and laughter are profoundly powerful tools of expression and healing. Laughter, in particular, helps release feelings of discomfort, embarrassment, anxiety and fear. Just like tears and raging, children often try to use these processes to help them release painful feelings and to process and heal from uncomfortable, stressful and traumatic experiences. Yet, in this culture, we don't always understand these natural forms of expression.

- Children who laugh if we're being harsh are not 'laughing at us' or 'being disrespectful'; they're trying to express and release feelings of fear.

- Children who are being silly and goofy after school aren't being 'manic'; they're trying to express and release feelings of discomfort from doing new things and feeling confused and overwhelmed.

- Children who are being playful before bed are not 'winding themselves up' or 'fighting sleep'; they're trying to express feelings from the day so that they can feel relaxed enough to sleep.

As parents, we can both cooperate with these natural healing, relaxation and expression processes that children invite us towards, and we can also bring precise games in to support our child in these processes if needed. For this purpose, Aletha Solter developed attachment play, which consists of nine types of play that can be used in different parenting scenarios to help children heal, learn, and process painful feelings that are causing unenjoyable behaviours.

We have a deep trust that children know what they need to come 'back into balance' (to use Lael's terminology). Play is often one of the most powerful languages children understand to process what is happening in their lives. You may find that your four-year-old who has just started kindergarten comes home and wants to play kindergarten. They might set up a game and role-play what has happened for them. This is a powerful inbuilt process to make sense and heal from all that has happened in their day. Or, if your child hasn't spent much time with you or you have been away, they may playfully want to climb all over you or play some sort of body contact game to connect with you after being separated. Or, if your family is having another baby, your older child may come to terms with the changes in your family by initiating games where they are a baby and want to be taken care of. Wrapping them up in a blanket and cooing over them may elicit giggles and laughter, which helps them to release the feelings they have as they imagine what having a new sibling might mean for them.

A wonderful example of a child healing and making sense of her experience was when Lael's youngest daughter broke her arm when she was eight and needed several x-rays and medical intervention. Healing from trauma not only involves expressing feelings and tension, it also involves helping children feel powerful where they originally felt powerless. Here, she got to play the powerful role where she was in charge of what was happening. Lael says, 'Even though I had done a great deal of listening to her feelings in relation to this situation, a few weeks after the incident, my daughter set up a game in the lounge room called "x-rays". She set up an x-ray room, complete with a clothes horse that became the x-ray machine. After an elaborate set-up of props and different toys, my daughter became the radiographer and x-rayed everyone. My daughter played this game on and off for a week with anyone who came to the house.'

There are hundreds of games and ways that children use this natural healing process, and often all that is needed is willingness to play with them. They will often do the rest. You might want to ask them, 'Hey, do you want to play for half an hour? We can do anything you like.' And then be curious about what game they want to play. You might be surprised at the wonderful insights you receive into their world and what they might be coming to terms with and healing from.

Attachment play can also be used when a child is feeling agitated. Coming in close and being silly, making strange noises, and inviting your child into a wrestling game where they can be stronger and regain some power are wonderful ways to build connection and use laughter to help release built-up feelings and emotions. Sometimes a little silliness goes a long way. Children usually love it when their parents are being goofy, and the laughter that comes can be a wonderful guide to let you know you are on the healing path. As adults, we might find ourselves really enjoying this play too. In this culture, we often disconnect from our natural ability to play and be silly as we become adults. Using attachment play with our children can help to keep us playful or to return to playfulness and invites laughter to also bring its healing magic to us.

## Loving Limits

In authoritarian parenting, limits are harsh and punitive, designed to create fear in children which then stops them from doing what we don't want them to do. In permissive parenting, limits tend to be absent. In Aware Parenting, we offer both Limits and Loving Limits (a term devised by Marion). Limits are when we say no to something based on our own needs in that moment. Loving Limits are when we say no to our child's behaviour that is caused by accumulated feelings, and we say yes to those feelings that lie underneath the behaviour. Loving Limits are particularly helpful in response to a child's aggression and agitation (although they can be used with suppression too).

*'Loving Limits say no to a child's behaviour and yes to the underlying feelings causing that behaviour.'*
~ Marion

When we stay calmly centred, we can stop aggression and then listen to the feelings causing it. When we offer a Loving Limit, we are supporting children to move to the healthy expression of crying and raging until they come out the other side feeling calm, relaxed, and freer from the feelings that caused the behaviour in the first place.

We can offer that Loving Limit when they are throwing something at their sister, pulling the dog's tail, or refusing to get off the iPad.

Or perhaps your child is agitated, and they keep asking for things. Even after you have responded to their apparent need, perhaps by cutting the bread differently or offering a selection of drinks, they still have a whiny tone. Or maybe your tween asks for a new pair of shoes but then wants the socks, jeans and top to go with them, and no matter what you have bought, they don't feel a sense of fulfilment.

When nothing is helping your child feel satisfied, underlying feelings are often the cause. This is because their feelings and behaviour are not caused by unmet needs, but by accumulated painful feelings from the past. These types of behaviour can be a child's way of asking for a catalyst to express their brewing feelings in the form of a Loving Limit. A calm, clear, compassionate 'no' can give the support they need to express their feelings such as outrage, disappointment or frustration. To offer a Loving Limit, we need to be relatively calm in our body and we can then offer empathy from there. 'I hear that you don't enjoy the bread cut in any of these ways, and I'm not willing to make you any more sandwiches, darling,' and then listen to the upset feelings emerge. Or we might respond to our tween with, 'Sweetheart, I hear that you want these things, and I'm only willing to buy the shoes today.'

Do you ever notice yourself expecting your child to respond to your 'no' with 'Okay, I understand, no problem?' But how often do we even respond that way as an adult? When you feel frustrated, do you reply with, 'Thank you for expressing a limit and saying no to me; I shall take that on board and process all my feelings without expressing them to you?' Have you ever found yourself in that situation feeling frustrated or angry, perhaps even thinking, 'It's not fair' or 'How could they do that to me?' Yet, we expect children to hear a Loving Limit, accept it and move on. Remember that the Loving Limit isn't just about saying no to the behaviour. It's also about saying yes to the feelings underneath the behaviour. The Loving Limit is the loving place that they can push up against which facilitates a release of those feelings.

Our role in expressing the Loving Limit is to offer it calmly and compassionately and then hold the space for whatever feelings may arise. Sometimes the words they then express will be about the sandwiches or how unfair it is to not have the same jeans as everyone else. No matter the words, continuing to offer empathy and understanding for the feelings creates a safe environment for the child to feel, express and release their underlying feelings. They will generally come out the other side calmer and brighter, and we can see so clearly at these times that the Loving Limit has facilitated the release that the child needs.

The tone and calmness with which we express this Loving Limit are so important. If we yell, get angry or become forceful, we have moved into power-over our child. Later in the book, you'll find more ways that support you to be calm and centred so you can offer true Loving Limits.

In the next six chapters, we will explore various scenarios based on what we've talked about so far with more in-depth information and examples to give you a clear idea of how you can actually put Aware Parenting into practice. Although this all might sound easy in theory, having all this information isn't always enough to respond in ways that we want to as parents. Otherwise, we'd all just turn on the Aware Parenting switch! We invite you to be compassionate with yourself and remember that we cannot necessarily change our behaviour just through cognitive understanding unless the cause of the behaviour is simply a lack of information.

Just like your child/ren, if your behaviour is due to unmet needs or painful feelings, you won't be able to change it through thoughts and information alone. Often our own unmet needs and painful feelings from past stress and trauma will get in the way of offering connection and listening, attachment play, or Loving Limits.

In Part III, in Reparenting Ourselves, we'll explore ways that we can meet our needs and feel and heal painful feelings as adults, so you can feel connected and compassionate with your child more of the time.

Understanding Children's Feelings

# Part II
# Responses to Everyday Parenting Challenges

'Our children want to cooperate, be gentle and sleep when they're tired. They are not deliberately doing things that we don't enjoy. They need our help. Aware Parenting offers that help.'

~ Marion

CHAPTER 4

# Not Cooperating and Not Listening

*'Spencer, it's time to have a bath. Would you pack up your LEGO?'
Spencer's mum shouts from the kitchen.*

*Four-year-old Spencer is deeply engrossed in building a LEGO tower. With a lot of concentration, he's built it really high, and in this moment, it's the only thing happening in his world. He can hear his mum saying something, but he's not really listening because he's focusing intently on finding four more green pieces for the top of this tricky red piece.*

*'Spencer, I've asked you twice already! Please pack up what you are doing. I want you to get into the bath! It's getting late.'*

*Spencer is feeling excited. He managed to click in those four pieces, and now he has an idea that if he balances the big blue one on the end, it will look like a big ship.*

*'Spencer! That is it! I'm sick of asking! You are not listening to what I am saying. The LEGO is going away until tomorrow night. You are making me so angry!'*

*Spencer's mum has been yelling these commands from the kitchen. In Spencer's world, that is another world away, as he is deeply engrossed in his extraordinary creation. He hears something about a bath, but it is of no interest as he just wants to see how high he can build this and if it could look like a big ship.*

*Spencer's mum is now standing beside him, and he can sense she is angry. She picks up the box of LEGO to put it on the high shelf, and Spencer lets out a loud protest. 'No! I am playing with it! No! Mummy!'*

> *Spencer's mum is frustrated and annoyed. She wants to get her son in the bath and then into bed so he can get up in the morning on time. She's telling herself that he 'never listens' and is doing this 'deliberately' and that he 'made her' angry. 'Why does he always do this?' she's thinking.*

Spencer's mum needs cooperation and ease and desperately wants to sit down and rest after a long day. She's feeling tired and frustrated. Nothing has gone to plan for her today. Spencer feels deeply powerless and upset as his beautiful unfinished LEGO creation is taken away from him. Emotional tension is in the air for them both.

Here, we see Spencer not doing what his mother asked him to do. Have you ever found yourself in a similar position as Spencer? Perhaps your partner or friend is asking you to do something when you're engrossed in finishing an email that requires concentration, or you're on the very last episode of a season finale. When we put ourselves in our child's shoes, this can help us respond in empathic and effective ways when they aren't cooperating with us. There are two key ways in which we might experience our child not cooperating with us: 1) when we want them to do something, and they're not doing it, or 2) when we want them to stop doing something, and they're not stopping.

## Why Children Don't Cooperate

From an Aware Parenting perspective, if we want to help our child/ren listen and cooperate with us, we need to understand why they don't and what they need from us to help them so that they are willing to cooperate. We can see why this is so different from other parenting paradigms.

An authoritarian paradigm wouldn't consider a child's felt experience or willingness. The focus would be on what the parent can do to make the child do what they want, and they might use coercion, force and threats to achieve that. (Again, we invite you to have compassion for yourself if you notice yourself doing that with your child/ren. When we grow up in this paradigm, we can easily fall into acting in these ways when we feel powerless.) By contrast, in permissive parenting, we'd probably give up on what we were asking our child to do (and probably get resentful, perhaps even lashing out with harsh words later that day).

You might find it helpful to look to your experience to help understand what is going on for your child/ren. For example, if your boss said with a tense body posture, from the other side of the office, without looking at you: 'Right, today you have to do this new project. You must start it now. Bring it to me when you've finished it.' How would you feel, especially if you had no interest in the project? But how about if your boss came up to your desk, made eye contact, and said, with a warm tone, a relaxed posture, and a calm presence: 'Hi! How are you today? Guess what! That new project came in for us to do today. I know you aren't interested in this campaign; I do understand – I find it pretty boring too! So I was wondering how we could make it fun. I've asked Polly if she is willing to join in, and I thought we could all do it together. I've brought superfood smoothies, and I thought we could have some breaks just to get through it. The company really want it done today. Would you be willing to join us? I'd really appreciate your presence.' How would you feel? Would you be more likely to be willing?

Sometimes we forget that children are human beings too and that many things that are important to us are not important to them. Often, we ask them to do things because of our needs or because of cultural conditioning and societal norms, as well as our needs for their safety and wellbeing. None of these may be of any interest to them!

## How We Can Help Children Cooperate

Just like us, children are much more likely to be willing to cooperate with us in doing something we want them to do if they:

- Understand the reason for our request.
- Feel connected with us and experience that we care about them and their needs.
- Have a sense of choice and autonomy.
- Are feeling relatively relaxed. If they're feeling tense and have painful feelings bubbling, it's going to be very hard for them to be willing to cooperate.

You might recognise that this takes into account the list of causes of behaviour that we shared earlier in the book: thoughts, needs and feelings.

Continuing with the example of how we might feel in a workplace situation. If we feel stressed and are experiencing criticism, our willingness to do some extra work or help a colleague is likely to be minimal. We may help out, but begrudgingly. In the same way, understanding how to help your child feel relaxed and happy – through attachment play and listening to accumulated painful feelings – helps them feel more calm and comfortable and more connected with their natural willingness to cooperate.

All aspects of Aware Parenting help us understand the importance of giving a child information (whilst knowing that this is just one aspect of eliciting cooperation). It prioritises a warm, loving and respectful connection between parent and child. It supports the child's needs for autonomy and choice; and the healthy expression of feelings through supported laughter, crying, and tantrums (so that children can feel relaxed and happy more of the time and find it easier to cooperate with us).

So, let's go back to the scenario between Spencer and his mum, looking through this lens.

If we look at things from Spencer's perspective, he is fully immersed in what, to him, is his 'work'. His focus on building the greatest big ship that his imagination can dream up is as important to him as when we are in the middle of an important project. When we remember how *we* feel in that experience, we are more likely to respond to our child in ways that help him experience being understood and cared about, which are part of the keys to cooperation.

However, this doesn't mean we ignore ourselves as parents. Spencer's Mum could connect with these three aspects in herself – what she's thinking, needing and feeling. Instead of telling herself that Spencer is deliberately not cooperating to 'make her mad,' she might choose to remember that he isn't doing it deliberately and has deeper reasons for his actions. She probably needs cooperation, ease and harmony. She might be feeling tired and be looking forward to Spencer going to bed so she can have a rest, connect with her partner, exercise or focus on her own projects. Valuing her own needs as important, as well as Spencer's needs, will make a difference in how she responds. She may also realise that she's feeling frustrated because when he doesn't respond, his behaviour helps her connect with feelings from times at work when she wasn't heard, and those feelings of frustration and anger bubble up towards him. If Spencer's Mum connects in compassionately with her own needs and feelings first, she might then feel the presence in her body to connect with Spencer. Connecting with him means that he feels that connection and care, which will help him find it easier to move away from what he's doing into having a bath.

She might move closer to him, sit beside him on the floor, gently put her hand on his back with her loving presence, and offer some connection. 'Wow! I love what you're building! Would you like to tell me about it?' As Spencer shares with her his passion for his creation, his Mum could stay present for a few minutes and contribute to his needs for connection and care so that he knows that his needs matter to her and that she's interested in what he's interested in.

Next, she might focus on the information piece – letting him know what she wants. 'Hey, sweetheart! In about ten minutes, I want you to hop in the bath.'

And then, she could move to the choice part of the list and offer him a choice about this next action. 'Would you like to leave this here so you can return to it tomorrow, or would you like to move it to the table?' She might offer him choices about how to get to the bath. 'Would you like to walk to the bath, or would you like a piggyback?'

And remember the next thing on the list? If Spencer has feelings about leaving his LEGO, then some attachment play might help him release any light feelings of powerlessness or frustration through laughter and play. 'Captain Spencer, I am a magical motorboat from your LEGO world! Would you like to climb on my back, fasten your motorboat seatbelt, and we can zoom as fast as we can to the magical water world bathroom waiting for you? Captain Spencer, how fast do you want the motorboat to go? Zooooomm...'

When we offer children information, connection, choice and fun, they are far more likely to cooperate. Just like we are much more likely to be willing to say yes if we're given these experiences.

## Helping Children with Safety, Health and Wellbeing

As parents of younger children, we so often want them to do things that are about their safety or health or wellbeing, which they often may not understand. These are common places for conflict, such as getting into the car seat, brushing teeth or getting dressed.

> *Three-year-old Stella refuses to get in her car seat and makes her body rigid and as stiff as a board as her mum tries to put her in. All she really wants to do is sit in the front seat and push all the buttons and pretend to drive. Stella's mum might try pleading with her, offering her some chocolate if she is a 'good girl' and gets into her seat. Or she may count to three and say, 'If you don't get into your car seat, we won't be able to go to the park later on.'*

Rewards and punishments sometimes work, but often they have painful consequences in the short term because the deeper underlying reasons for not cooperating aren't addressed. In the long term, they often deleteriously affect the parent-child relationship and also lose their power because the child becomes more powerful.

For three-year-olds, powerlessness is a common experience. Whenever they are told what to do, made to do things they don't really want to do and are learning about a world they can't control, it is natural for them to feel powerless.

In Stella's situation of not wanting to get into the car seat, her mum could:

1. Notice her thoughts and avoid thinking that Stella is being annoying or manipulative. Instead, she can remind herself that all children have needs for autonomy and choice and that accumulated feelings of powerless can make it hard for a child to be willing to cooperate.
2. Connect in compassionately with herself by feeling into her willingness for both of them to get their needs met. She might give herself a moment of self-empathy about needing ease and cooperation. Having connected in with herself, it will be easier to connect with Stella in a way that Stella can really feel, thus meeting her child's needs for connection and care.
3. She might give Stella some information: 'I really want for us to go home so I can make dinner and we can hang out before bed. Remember that the car seat keeps you safe whilst Mummy is driving.'
4. She might then offer choices, 'Would you like to climb in yourself, or would you like me to pick you up, sweetie?'
5. She may play some fun games by trying to sit in the car seat and pretending to be surprised that it's too small, or give Stella a toy steering wheel so she can pretend to drive from her car seat.
6. She may offer a Loving Limit to Stella and calmly let her know that she wants Stella to sit in the car seat and then listen to her feelings. She may stay calm and offer empathy as Stella expresses her powerlessness about sitting in the car seat.

## Asking Our Children to Stop Doing Something

Let's look at another scenario, this time when a parent wants their child to stop doing something.

> *Here we see five-year-old Charlie throwing the ball at the wall. He knows his parents don't want him to throw the ball inside, but he feels agitated and annoyed. His dad sees him and says, 'Charlie, we don't throw balls inside! Take it outside if you want to throw it.'*
>
> *Charlie looks at his dad and throws the ball harder at the wall, and as he does it, he lets out a little laugh. Charlie's dad feels his anger rising and says, 'Charlie! I've told you already, no throwing balls at the wall!'*
>
> *Charlie's nervous laughter gets louder. His dad is thinking all kinds of things: 'Why doesn't he respect me? He thinks this is funny! He's laughing at me. He won't do what I'm telling him. He's so disrespectful.' As he starts to walk towards Charlie, Charlie laughs louder and throws the ball at his dad's face, hitting him on the nose.*
>
> *Charlie's dad lets out a loud yell, and Charlie runs away, laughing as he runs.*

Is this scenario familiar to you? Have you ever asked your child to stop doing something and they continue to do it, or maybe they do that thing even more? Has your child ever laughed in this kind of situation? Have you ever told yourself judgemental things about why they are doing that? Have you ever felt frustrated and angry and responded in harsh or power-over ways?

Again, let's return to the three causes of behaviour list and look at this for ourselves as parents and then for our children.

1. What we're thinking.
2. What we're needing.
3. What we're feeling.

If we have any of the following thoughts about why our child is doing things, we're likely to feel frustrated, angry, or powerless:

- 'They're doing it deliberately.'
- 'They never do what I ask.'
- 'They are disrespectful.'
- 'They are doing it to wind me up.'
- 'They are [*insert judgement here*].'
- 'They think this is funny!'
- 'They lack empathy.'
- 'They don't realise how serious this is!'

This is why understanding the Aware Parenting theory is so important. When we understand why a child is acting a certain way, we are more likely to think compassionate thoughts and thus feel calmer and be more able to respond with empathy in effective ways.

## Why Do Children Often Laugh in These Kinds of Scenarios?

As we explored in a previous chapter, laughter is one of the ways that we express and release feelings of embarrassment, fear, uncertainty and discomfort. If you've ever remembered laughing in a situation where you feel uncomfortable, that will again help you put yourself in your child's shoes. Laughter in these situations is generally a child expressing and releasing fear, especially if we have reacted in harsh ways in the past, and they're trying to heal from that fear by releasing it. Understanding this can help us feel compassionate towards our child/ren when they are laughing, rather than frustrated and angry.

## Why Do Children Do What We Don't Want Them to Do?

Instead of telling ourselves judgemental things about why a child is doing something we've asked them not to do, Aware Parenting has a compassionate perspective. There are generally three key reasons why children do things we've asked them not to.

The first is that they are doing something that meets their needs, such as learning, competence or play. We might be interrupting that and suggesting something that doesn't meet their needs at all. When we connect in with what needs they are aiming to meet, we can often find ways for both our child and ourselves to get our needs met.

The second is that they have painful accumulated feelings, and they need our help to express them through crying and healthy raging. They are specifically wanting help to let the feelings out, so they do things that they know we don't want them to do. That's a flag for feelings. They are saying to us (in a very hidden code!), 'I am feeling lots of really uncomfortable feelings right now, and I need your help to let them out. Would you please help me? I will keep doing this thing so that you can lovingly stop me and listen to the feelings that are trying to burst out of my body.' Here they are requesting a Loving Limit.

The third, less common reason is that we have been unclear about this behaviour in the past, and they want clear and consistent (and compassionate) information about whether we are willing for this to happen or not. Here they are asking for a clear Limit, as we express our 'no'.

Understanding what they are really wanting means we are more likely to be able to respond, either with finding a way for both of us to get our needs met, or a clear Limit, if they were wanting our authentic 'no'; or with a Loving Limit, if they had painful feelings driving their behaviour.

## Loving Limits

If we've already ascertained that giving the child information or aiming to meet their needs hasn't changed their behaviour, then we can generally tell that the cause of the behaviour is painful accumulated feelings.

With Loving Limits, we see that the behaviour is caused by painful feelings. We aim to stop the behaviour lovingly and listen to the underlying feelings that are causing the behaviour. We are saying a loving 'no' to the behaviour and a loving 'yes' to the feelings that are causing the behaviour. This is what differentiates Aware Parenting from more old-fashioned parenting paradigms. Offering a Loving Limit involves the following:

1. We understand the underlying cause of the behaviour.
2. We stop the behaviour with loving compassion and without harshness, shaming or disconnection.
3. We provide the conditions to support the child to express the underlying feelings.
4. We listen to those painful feelings with loving compassion.

There are a few keys to offer Loving Limits effectively, and the first one is to stay relatively calm in our body and feelings whilst offering the Loving Limit. Instead of telling the child to stop doing something from across the room, we can come in close and connect with them. We can look them in the eye, get down on their level and perhaps even hold their arm or hand gently if they don't stop when we ask. We can use the minimum physical action to stop the behaviour. Our actions let the child know that we are not willing for them to continue that behaviour. When we can offer that Loving Limit with calm empathy, we create a safe container for the child to protest against.

And remember, that is the real reason for their behaviour in the first place – the flag for feelings – the call for help to express the underlying feelings. Holding this in mind is important because we are not just offering the Loving Limit to stop the behaviour. We are using it to stop the behaviour AND then listen to the underlying feelings causing it.

Returning to the scenario of Charlie refusing to put down the ball. Charlie's dad could put his hand on his son's hand that's holding the ball, using the minimum pressure to prevent it from being thrown, and then calmly say, 'I'm not willing for you to throw the ball inside the house, Charlie, and I'm here and I'm listening.' This creates an edge for Charlie to push up against to offload those feelings of agitation. When a Loving Limit is given, and the child feels emotionally safe because the adult isn't using power-over, the child has an opportunity to release their pent-up feelings. Once Charlie has had the opportunity to rage, cry and release the agitation, his body will be restored to its natural sense of calm, and he will be more able to listen and cooperate.

## Family Meetings

For older children and teenagers, family meetings are an important way to elicit cooperation. When families regularly gather together and each person, whatever their age, gets to express unmet needs, everyone in the family can get heard and together can find creative solutions. Perhaps fourteen-year-old Kellie isn't ever willing to do any washing up or putting out of the rubbish when her parents ask her to and they are feeling overwhelmed and frustrated and would really like some help. They might be tempted to give threats that they will prevent her from seeing her friends unless she does more to help around the house, but this will only create deeper disconnection and resentment for both parent and teenager. Instead of trying to make her do things with threats, coercion or punishment, they could discuss their needs in a family meeting, listen to her responses, and all together find ways for everyone to get their needs met. This is also an opportunity for her to express things that she's not happy with or would like help with. This is a truly democratic way to parent, because everyone's needs and feelings matter and are considered.

*Remember: A child's natural state is to be connected to us, and when they feel that, they are more likely to want to cooperate with and contribute to us.*

**CHAPTER 5**

# Feelings and Tears and Tantrums

*Five-year-old Millie hears her mum coming down the hallway. She's snuggled up in bed, warm and cosy, role-playing a conversation between her two teddies. As her mum enters the room, she turns the light on and says, 'Good morning, Millie Moo, time to get up, or you'll be late for school. What do you want to wear today, shorts or a skirt? Which colour top are you going to put on? Come on, honey, I still have all the lunches to make.'*

*Millie is happily engrossed in her game with her two teddies and doesn't want to get up for school. She often feels frustrated hearing all the questions in the morning. The frustration starts to build as tension in her body.*

*After Millie gets dressed and comes downstairs, she's asked more questions about what she wants to eat for breakfast. She doesn't want to answer because she's not hungry and she's engrossed in playing with the dog. Her puppy loves belly rubs in the morning. Millie's mum asks for the fourth time what she wants for breakfast from over in the kitchen, with a sharp edge to her voice. Millie registers the tone, and a little bit more tension builds in her little body. She doesn't like the rush of school mornings.*

*Mum is trying to get Millie's three-year-old brother to put on his shoes so they can get in the car, but he doesn't really want to cooperate. He wants to wear gumboots, even though it's going to be hot. Millie can hear her Mum getting more frustrated. Although Millie knows her mum is trying her best to stay calm, mornings are always a bit tense for everyone. Millie wishes her little brother would hurry up. She doesn't like being late to school. A little bit more tension accumulates.*

*As Millie walks into her classroom, she can't find her teacher Miss Burton. She loves Miss Burton, who is gentle and kind and helps her feel safe. Another lady walks up to her and introduces herself as Mrs Walsh. She is the fill-in teacher for the day because Miss Burton is away sick. Millie feels unsure. She doesn't know this other lady, and she feels a bit wary. She looks around for her mum for some reassurance, but Mum has already gone to drop off her brother. Millie has a funny feeling in her tummy.*

*As the day progresses, Mrs Walsh grumbles at some children for not doing what she asks. At one point, Millie needs to go to the toilet and puts up her hand to ask. Mrs Walsh tells her to wait as it is almost break time. She can go in ten minutes when the bell goes. Millie feels a bit panicked. She really needs to go to the toilet now, and she feels worried whether she can hang on or not. A little more tension builds in her body.*

*At break time, Millie runs to the toilet and is relieved that she gets there in time. But in doing that, she now doesn't know where her friends are playing. She walks around the playground looking for them, feeling a bit scared. The school is big with many kids, and she still feels a bit nervous around the bigger children. She sees a group of kids she knows and asks them if they know where her friends are playing. One of the kids yells, 'You have no friends!'*

*Millie replies, 'Yes, I do, I just can't find them!' but inside, she feels more tension brewing. She didn't like hearing that boy say that to her. Millie finds her friends in the sandpit, and before long, they're laughing and playing. She loves being with her friends. As the bell goes, they run to their classroom, and they run inside.*

*An adult shouts, 'No running inside!' Millie feels that knot in her belly again. She didn't mean to run. She was just caught up in the excitement with her friends.*

Mrs Walsh gives them an exercise to do with writing letters. Millie likes writing. She likes practising the shapes and drawing faces and hands and feet on the letters. She thinks they look cute when you turn them into people. As Mrs Walsh walks around the classroom to check what they are doing, she tells Millie to stop drawing on the letters and just write as instructed. Millie feels embarrassed. She lowers her head, her body feels small, and the tension becomes even bigger.

When the bell rings for the end of school, Millie scans the playground for her mum. She sees her mum talking to someone and runs over to hug her mum. Mum gives her a quick cuddle and sends her off to play on the playground so she can finish her conversation. Millie really wants to be close to her mum after such a big day, but she tries to find a friend to play with.

After picking up her little brother and finally getting home, her Mum tells them she has a surprise. 'On my lunch break today, I walked past a shop and saw these sparkly stickers, and I got some. Would you like them?'

'Yes!' Millie shouts, but her younger brother grabs the ones she wants. He was standing closer to Mum and took them before she could get there. Millie takes one look at this situation and explodes. 'I want those ones!' she yells at the top of her voice. She is screaming now: 'Give them to ME!' She launches forward to rip them out of her brother's hand, and he starts to run away, yelling, 'No, mine!' Millie is now feeling intense and big feelings of powerlessness, frustration and overwhelm from all those moments of stress throughout the day.

## Understanding the Accumulation of Feelings

Let's pause the story and ask, what is happening for Millie?

As the day unfolded, you can see the build-up of tension – from feeling rushed to unsure, embarrassed and powerless – building in her little body. When she arrives home – the place that feels safest and with the person that provides that safety – the feelings that have been pushed down all day bubble up and burst out. Not getting the stickers she wanted is the perfect balance of attention (a core concept in Aware Parenting) that brings her feelings to the surface.

An authoritarian parenting response might include yelling at Millie, and shaming her for being 'disrespectful, ungrateful and rude'. Punishment and power-over might include sending her to her room for a time out, telling her there will be no chocolate after dinner, or informing her that her brother now gets to keep all the stickers because she didn't express gratitude for them.

A permissive parenting response might include trying to make everything smooth again. Pleading with Millie's younger brother to just give her the stickers or offering Millie something that is a bigger gift than the stickers to see if that would help her feel happy again. Perhaps there might be an offer to drive back to the shop and get another pack of stickers.

You may see from both these parenting styles that they are not responding to the underlying cause of Millie's feelings. Punishing Millie doesn't help Millie's body to come back into balance. It actually adds to more stress and tension and sends a message that when she gets upset, love is withdrawn, and thus, that she is loved conditionally. After regular experiences like this, children learn that to get love from their parents, they need to suppress emotions that the parents deem 'negative'. This can have detrimental effects on a child, as they can internalise harsh self-judgements, which affect their attachment status and ability to express, process and understand emotions. They might come to believe that they will get hurt or rejected when they are upset, which might show up in them not expressing their feelings in future friendships and relationships.

The permissive response to Millie's outburst would send a different message. When Millie's mum moves into fixing or trying to 'make it better', she is communicating, 'Your feelings are too big for me.' This way of responding to the feelings doesn't address the reason for the feelings. It inadvertently communicates the same belief as authoritarian parenting does – 'your feelings are not welcome here.'

So how might we respond to this situation from an Aware Parenting perspective?

We could pause and see behind the behaviour. When tantrums and rage arrive, it is often a sign that feelings have accumulated to the point that a child can no longer hold in those feelings. The ability to speak clearly and calmly isn't available. The prefrontal cortex has gone offline, and the amygdala (centre of emotions within the brain) is in full fight or flight mode (see Chapter 3). When this happens, a child's ability to make decisions, rationalise and listen becomes very limited. However, unlike other approaches, we do not – even subtly – believe that children are lesser because of this. Nor are they pitied, shamed or belittled for expressing these feelings. In contrast, Aware Parenting sees the beauty, wisdom and healthiness of their emotional expression. Their body is involved in a natural process of homeostasis, where through crying and raging with loving support, a child moves from fight/flight and the associated feelings, to return to a state of calm and relaxation again.

A child's prefrontal cortex doesn't fully develop until around twenty-five years old (some even say twenty-nine). The prefrontal cortex is the part of the brain that is responsible for rational thinking and problem solving and plays a central role in cognitive control functions. By adulthood, some of us have learnt to express our emotions in words. However, in this culture, which demonises the expression of feelings rather than honouring their wisdom, much of what we have learnt to do is simply suppressing our feelings or dissociating from them. We can learn from children how to reconnect with the beauty and healing power of expressing our feelings through crying and raging in healthy ways.

Younger children are still in touch with their natural healing processes of crying and raging. However, babies and children learn how to respond to their own feelings and emotions from the responses of the adults around them. From this they also learn about how safe they are to express feelings and how welcome their emotions are.

> *In an ideal world, Millie's mum would be calm and relaxed when Millie started to express big feelings. She would take action to keep everyone safe, such as getting in between Millie and her brother. She might say, 'I'm here to keep everyone safe,' which can be a helpful communication not only to her children but also to her inner child. She may turn her attention to Millie and describe what she is seeing. 'I can see you are really upset, sweetheart. I'm listening.'*
>
> *Millie may try to grab her brother or the stickers, and Millie's mum would ideally stay calm and keep making sure no one gets hurt. Millie may push up against her or struggle to try and get her brother. Millie's mum may offer more empathy: 'I can see how frustrated you are, darling. I'm not willing for you to hit your brother. I'm here, and I'm listening.' (This is a classic Loving Limit).*
>
> *Millie may scream things like, 'It's not fair! I want those ones' or 'I hate you. Let me have the stickers I want!'*

In offering this Loving Limit, we are holding space for the feelings. We are aiming to be the calm in the storm. When we look behind the behaviour and assume that Millie has had a hard day at school, we welcome the big feelings as a process for Millie to offload some of the powerlessness she has felt. (As an aside, Lael's kids, who all went to mainstream schools, would express some version of this most days when picking them up in the early years. In the more mainstream education system, children often feel powerlessness, so it's very normal for young children to exhibit these types of releases.)

When we can stay calm and anchored in amongst our child's big feelings, they feel safe to let the feelings out and express themselves. Sometimes this might be a five-minute process, sometimes fifty minutes or more, depending on the severity and length of time of the stresses or mini-traumas they've experienced. The important message we are communicating is: 'Your feelings are not too much for me. I've got you. You're safe with me. I can hold all of these big feelings whilst you express them. I trust you and your feelings and your body.' This gives the child the core belief that their parent or caregiver sees and welcomes all of them and that they are safe when they feel big feelings.

> *As Millie's mum holds the storm while Millie offloads the stressors of the day, her rage and frustration transform into the next layer of feelings, and her tears. Her body softens. She climbs onto her mum's lap and starts to sob. She starts sharing that she found it hard at school because her teacher wasn't there. Millie tells her mum about not being able to go to the toilet when she wanted and how she really wanted to write her letters in the way she wanted to.*
>
> *As Millie expresses these big feelings, her mother listens, nods and offers sounds of empathy, holding the space for her daughter to share her woes. Millie's mum doesn't try and offer solutions or fix the issues during the expression, she just listens. More action generally isn't necessary, since children can think clearly after a big cry or rage, but if at the end of Millie's sharing she thinks this is required, she might add, 'Thank you for sharing with me, sweetheart, let me know if you want some ideas or help with any of those things.'*
>
> *Millie looks at her mum with fresh eyes and a relaxed body and says, 'Thanks for the stickers, Mum, let's make a big poster together.' Millie is now willing to share and play with her little brother, and her behaviour is naturally gentle and cooperative.*

You may have experienced a similar scenario with your child over the wrong-coloured cup or cutting their toast a certain way. This can also happen for teenagers after a stressful day at school, perhaps when there's a change of plans and you can no longer drive them to their friend's house. Whenever we see this big explosion of emotions, our first thought can be, 'Their feelings have overflowed.' We want our default setting as a parent to know that our task is to be calm in the storm. To be the safe place for those feelings to be expressed.

Now that may sound like a simple and easy thing to do. However, it is often the most challenging thing because of our own childhoods and daily stressors. In an ideal world, we would all hope to respond like Millie's mum did in the second scenario, staying calm and holding the space for her daughter to offload her feelings and return to a state of balance. In reality, this can require a lot from us to be able to do so.

## The Effects of Our Stresses

Let's take a look at how Millie's mum's day unfolded:

*As soon as the alarm goes off, the pressure is on. It's often a race against the clock to get two kids dressed, fed, bag packed and out the door by 8.15 a.m., so she can get to work on time. The kids are not cooperating even though she is trying to give them a choice about what they wear and what they eat. She tries to hurry them with a calm, caring voice, but she feels resentful that yet again, her partner isn't helping and she is left to do it all. He leaves early to go to the gym before work, so the morning hustle is all hers to wrestle with. Urgh!*

*Her son is having big feelings at daycare drop-off. He doesn't want her to go and starts crying, and she feels deep angst in her chest at leaving him. She doesn't enjoy her job and would prefer to be staying at home and having more relaxed time with her family but she doesn't even have time to feel these feelings and how much her life is not how she'd like it* to be. *As she races to work, someone cuts her off in traffic, and when she arrives at work, someone has parked in her designated space. Feeling frustrated, she drives around for another ten minutes to find a spot, and that means she's late for a meeting with her boss, that she was stressed about in the first place. Her boss is short with her for being late, and then she receives harsh feedback about a project that she had worked hard on. Then she finds she's somehow lost a vitally important document on her computer. Much like Millie, her levels of tension increase throughout the day.*

*As she races home to pick up the kids and start making dinner, she calls her partner and asks him to pick up some milk on the way home as they will need it in the morning.*

*At home, she decides to surprise the kids with some stickers, wanting to find a way to reconnect after her day at work, and Millie's reaction is big and loud. There are a lot of feelings being expressed, and she does her best to stay calm and centred for Millie, knowing that she has probably had a big day at school and needs to offload some tension.*

*As Millie calms down and she returns to making dinner, her partner arrives home, and as she greets him, she asks if he remembered to get the milk.*

*He replies with an apologetic 'Oh, sorry, I forgot!'*

*This is her tipping point, just like the stickers were for her daughter. She yells and slams her hand down on the counter! 'I asked you to get one thing, that's all! I do EVERYTHING around here!' Her partner is shocked as Millie's mum rages a bit more. She, too, is expressing the tensions of the day.*

*Now in an ideal world, Millie's mum wouldn't fly into a rage about the forgotten milk. She might say to her partner, 'I feel really frustrated, hearing that you haven't got the milk. But really, the frustration I'm feeling is from the really hard day I've had. I feel overwhelmed and stretched. Would you be willing to listen to me whilst I tell you some of the things that happened today and tell you about how frustrated I've felt?' However, for many adults, we didn't receive modelling of healthy expression of feelings. So often, we fly into our own unexpressed feelings when they have accumulated.*

*Children can often fulfil the role of being the straw that broke the camel's back when they don't do what we want, and we can often slip into rage from our own stresses or unmet needs and project them onto our children. We can see now how harsh it can be to place such high expectations on children to express their feelings in clear ways when so many adults still find it hard. But really, judgement or expectations are unnecessary and unhelpful, whatever our age. Compassion is the most helpful and healing response.*

The beauty of holding space for big feelings is that it helps children to stay connected with their natural capacity to express their feelings and through that, heal from stress and trauma and return to feeling relaxed and calm. If we offer a compassionate response, they also develop language to clearly communicate their feelings through words. But words do not replace the expression of feelings through crying and raging. As many of us weren't brought up in this paradigm of listening to emotions, it is something we need to relearn to be able to respond to our children in these ways.

You may also read Millie's story and feel sad seeing all the things she is experiencing each day, and also have compassion for Millie's mum, juggling children, work and family life. The stresses and scenarios mentioned are so common in our day-to-day lives. Understanding the effects of these environments on ourselves and our children can inspire us to make different choices wherever possible, to create less stress in our lives and in our children's lives. However, when we're not able to bring about change to stressful situations, we can always help our children process and heal from what they feel and the mini-traumas they encounter and thus support them to stay truly resilient.

*It's not about making them tough. It's about helping them naturally heal from stress, trauma and mini-traumas so they can return to their natural state of balance, from where they can meet the world with a clear mind and an open heart.*

## Listening to Frustration, Outrage and Tantrums

The usual list of three things can help us when our children are expressing big feelings:

### 1. *Telling ourselves helpful information*

- They are letting out feelings.
- They need my loving presence.
- They will feel more relaxed after this.
- These are the feelings that are causing the behaviour.
- They will be less likely to behave in ways I don't enjoy after this.
- They will know that their feelings are welcomed.

*What information would you like to remind yourself of when listening to their tears or tantrums?*

## 2. Meeting our needs

- Doing whatever we can to help ourselves feel comfortable – e.g. getting in a comfortable position.
- Feeling the support of the floor/chair/cushion.
- Connecting in with our knowing that we are safe and have power in this situation.
- Reminding ourselves that we are the parent and they are the child.
- Connecting with our breathing.
- Noticing physical details about them, e.g. the texture of their skin.
- In addition, the more we meet our needs on a day-to-day basis, the more present we will be.

*How would you like to meet your needs more at times like this and in general?*

## 3. Listening to our feelings

- That might be some silent self-empathy for how we're feeling.
- That might be reminding the younger parts of us that we will keep them safe.
- That might be noting that we'll send a message to our friend after this.
- That might be saying to our inner child, 'I'm here with you. I'm listening.'
- Again, the more we receive empathy or give ourselves empathy in general, the more spaciousness we are likely to have for listening to feelings.

*What would you find helpful when feelings bubble up for you at this time?*

## What Can We Do to Help When Our Child is Crying or Raging?

Letting them know that we are there with them, supporting them, listening, and loving them all help the crying or tantrum to be healing. We do this by offering eye contact, closeness, the continued Loving Limit if they need it, a loving tone of voice and compassionate words. 'I'm here with you. I'm listening. I understand.'

We can give them reassurance that we will stay with them until they've finished expressing their feelings and have moved out the other side. Once they have finished crying or raging, they might:

- Suddenly say, 'What's for dinner?'
- Want to cuddle up.
- Be particularly affectionate and loving.
- Fall asleep.
- Want to tell us about something painful that has happened.

We invite you to notice how your child is afterwards, compared to before the crying and raging. Noticing the difference in their expression, the tension in their muscles, how they concentrate, the amount of eye contact they make, the tone of their voice, how they sleep, and how they are with others can help reassure you that listening to the tears and tantrums is helpful. Remember how we talked about trying things out, observing what happens and taking that back to your next response? This is key in Aware Parenting. This makes you the powerful and connected parent that you are – listening to yourself and clearly observing your child. In all of these ways, they will tell you whether what you are doing is helpful or not.

How are you feeling, having read this?

## CHAPTER 6

# Aggression and Power-Over

*Luana's dad could hear some huffing and puffing coming from the playroom. 'I don't care if you had it first; it's mine! Auntie Paloma gave it to me. I won't let you touch it!'*

*Dad walks down the corridor to find nine-year-old Luana pulling on a skipping rope attached to five-year-old Felipe's foot. A struggle is happening, and Luana is using her size and power to get the skipping rope back. 'But I was just using it to be a rope on my ship,' Felipe exclaims.*

*Luana moves in with even more force. Her voice is getting louder, and her frustration is palpable. 'It's mine! Give it back! I never said you could use it,' she says as she yanks the skipping rope harder, and Felipe lets out a yelp. 'I am the boss of what we play. You have to ask me for whatever you want to touch.'*

*Luana and Felipe's dad is now standing in the doorway, watching this all unfold. It's only 8 a.m., and he feels exhausted already. 'How is the rest of the day going to be if it's like this already?' he wonders. He can see that Luana is activated and wants power over what is happening. His internal dialogue sounds like this; 'Why can't you guys just get along? It's only 8 a.m., and it's only a skipping rope. I'm sure we have another one somewhere. I am so over this bickering and Luana trying to control everything.' He's aware of these thoughts. He can acknowledge that in the past, his default may have been to start yelling straight away and telling them to share. He knows there is another way to support his children without having power-over. Using power-over her to try to stop her using power-over Felipe never made sense anyway!*

*As the fighting escalates, Luana's dad takes a deep breath, steps into the room and exclaims. 'Wow! It looks like a tug of war is happening in here! Can I play?' Both children pause for a second, registering that their dad is here and he is calm. The invitation to play and connect helps them both to soften.*

*'Come on, you guys. You two against me, let's do it!' Luana's need for connection is met, and her feelings feeding her need to control her brother subside. She helps Felipe unroll the rope around his leg and instructs him to hold the end tight together: 'Let's pull Dad over!'*

*Luana's dad knows she needs to feel more powerful, so he plays tug of war to help the kids feel that sense of power. He makes a point of falling over with mock surprise, so his kids feel stronger and then he pretends not to know how to pull the rope, so they need to show him how to do it (these are both power-reversal games from an Aware Parenting perspective). There's a lot of laughter, and both children feel calmer and more relaxed after fifteen minutes of play. The accumulated feelings of powerlessness in Luana that manifested in her needing to have power over her brother have now eased somewhat, but they haven't been entirely released.*

*A few hours after lunch, Luana and Felipe decide to play a game on the trampoline. They collect all the balls they can find and load them in so they can jump and bounce around. The first ten minutes of playing are full of shrieking, laughter, and squealing. The children are excited and having a wonderful time. In all the excitement, Felipe picks up a ball, and not realising his strength or close proximity to his sister, throws it at her, and it accidentally hits her in the face.*

*Luana lets out an enormous shriek; 'You hit me! You hit me in the face!' She's moved from zero to a hundred in a matter of seconds, and she throws herself on top of Felipe, hitting him with all her force.*

*Luana's dad springs to action from where he has been gardening and races over to break up the fight. In his mind, his instant reaction would be to grab Luana and fling her over to the other side of the trampoline with force. He can feel the fight/flight response in his body, and his inner thoughts go straight to protecting his son and punishing his daughter for causing harm.*

*Instead, as he unzips the trampoline and climbs inside, he uses his body to get between the children. Despite his initial internal reactivity, he knows it's important to bring some calm to the situation. Sitting between the children, he says, 'I'm here, I'm here to help. I'm sorry I didn't get here quicker. I'm sorry you've been hurt.'[5]*

*Once upon a time, his reaction would have been to punish and shame Luana for hitting. He would have sent her to her room and told her, 'We don't hit in this family!' believing that she would 'learn her lesson' about not hitting. But nowadays, he knows that Luana's reaction is caused by feelings – probably the same powerlessness that was spilling out earlier.*

*Luana has just started a new school, and there are many new things in her days there that she doesn't have much say over. Being told what to do and when to do it many times a day have led to the profound sense of powerlessness. These feelings have been surfacing in her trying to have control in other places in her life. Being hit in the face by the ball helped all those feelings of powerlessness come to the surface. The anger and rage she's been feeling all come tumbling out at that moment with her brother.*

*As Luana's dad hugs Felipe, he reaches out to touch Luana and says, 'I can see that you're outraged, and I am not willing to let you hurt your brother. I'm here to help.' Her dad senses that there are a lot more feelings that she needs to express. He asks Felipe if he would be willing to go inside and find his Mum for a cuddle whilst he helps Luana with her feelings.*

---

[5]. The phrase, 'I'm sorry I didn't get here in time' is from Patty Wipfler, founder of Hand in Hand Parenting.

*As Felipe moves inside for some closeness with his mum, Luana's dad directs his full attention to a seething Luana; 'I see that you're angry. I'm here. I'm listening.'*

*The invitation helps her connect more deeply to her feelings and she starts yelling, 'I'm not angry, get away from me!'*

*Her dad moves back a little but stays deeply present with her and says, 'I'm not going to leave you alone with these big feelings. I'm right here with you.'*

*This 'balance of attention' of the memory of being hit by the ball, along with her dad's closeness, words and willingness to hear her feelings bring even more emotions to the surface. Luana starts yelling more and thrashing her arms and legs on the trampoline. When her feet or fists get close to her dad, he moves his body to keep himself safe but stays right close and reassures her that he's still listening.*

*The raging continues for about ten minutes, and as Luana's dad offers more empathy, she starts crying. Luana's dad opens his arms to her, and she falls into them and then sobs deeply. After another ten minutes, Luana whispers, 'Daddy, I don't like how they tell me what to do all the time at school.'*

*Luana's dad listens and offers some gentle words; 'I hear you, sweetheart,' and welcomes her tears. After more tears, Luana's whole body relaxes as she melts into her dad, and he asks if there is more she would like to talk about. They discuss everything she finds painful at the new school and he says how sorry he is that she doesn't get to choose. Then they talk about what she might do to repair with her younger brother.*

*Luana, calm and relaxed now, and her dad, together go inside. She goes to get paper and pen from Mum whilst Luana's dad goes to connect with Felipe. He's been playing with his train set on the floor, and his dad is curious to see how he's feeling after the incident on the trampoline. As* he starts playing trains with Felipe, Luana walks in and hands Felipe a picture. 'Sorry for hitting you, Felipe. I know you didn't mean to throw the ball at me. I've made a drawing for you.'

Felipe looks at the picture and says, 'That's a dumb drawing. You are not even a good drawer.' Their dad registers the look on Luana's face and says, 'I really see you wanted to repair, honey, and I think Felipe may have some feelings here. I'm going to help him for a minute. Would you like to go back to Mum?'

Luana leaves the room, and Felipe says, 'She is such a poo, and she does dumb drawings. I hate her picture.' Felipe's dad holds in his awareness the general loving dynamic between his two children. They sometimes have fights and disagreements, but he knows they care deeply for each other. When one or the other is speaking harshly about their sibling, it's a sign that more feelings are sitting below the surface. In the past, he may have thought things like 'Oh, they will sort it out,' or, 'He doesn't mean it,' or he may have even said, 'You don't feel like that. You love your sister,' or, 'You shouldn't say things like that. Be nice.'

But now, he understands that Felipe may have some painful feelings after his sister's responses to him. He touches Felipe on the arm and says, 'Do you feel frustrated when Luana wants to decide what you play?' Felipe welcomes the invitation to speak about how he feels. 'Yes, I hate that she is the boss of playing, and I don't like her drawing and she hurt me!'

Felipe's dad listens and says, 'Yes, I hear you! What else?' He invites all of Felipe's feelings to be expressed, knowing that Luana is out of earshot, and welcomes his feelings about all that happened that day. After ten minutes of Felipe sharing about all the things he didn't like, his dad sees that Felipe feels much calmer and more connected. He's making eye contact, his muscles are more relaxed and he's snuggling up to his dad.

## Parenting with Compassion

After reading this story, you might think that sounds impossible and exhausting! Even though this story is fictional, we would love to let you know that responding like this is possible, AND we also send lots of compassion for all the times that things don't unfold like this. There may be times when Luana and Felipe's dad does yell or walk away. There may be times when he does feel powerless and moves into power-over. There may be times when he wants to have a beer in the afternoon and check out from all the holding and listening he has been doing! Do you resonate?

Parenting with awareness, calmness, and compassion is a skill that requires not only practice but also plenty of support. Perhaps at the end of the day, Luana and Felipe's dad does have a glass of wine while he unpacks the day with his partner and experiences being acknowledged and appreciated for all the emotional holding and listening he has done. Perhaps he goes for a run, catches up with a friend or does some journalling to fill up his cup so he can continue to be the generally calm anchor in his children's lives. Parenting this way is possible, but not if we don't take care of ourselves, access support and have our own feelings lovingly heard.

Anger is often the first place we go when we feel powerless, such as when things aren't working the way we want or when our children aren't doing what we ask. When our child starts doing things we specifically asked them not to do, we might feel really frustrated, and we might explode with anger.

When our child is agitated or aggressive, our role is to help the feelings underlying that behaviour be felt, expressed and released. We are aiming to support their aggression or agitation to transform into expression. But if we respond to our child's aggression with our own rage, then no one feels safe. Children will often shut down and dissociate if we yell or speak harshly from a place of anger. Then they not only have the original feelings that were causing the agitation or aggression still sitting inside, but now they have an added layer of painful feelings such as fear or powerlessness.

A child's core needs are attachment and connection. They will do whatever it takes to ensure they have that, even if that means shutting down how they feel. This is why authoritarian parenting can get immediate results but has painful short and long-term consequences for the relationship between parent and child.

Often the child's driving force for attachment, safety and belonging trumps their internal desire to be true to themselves.

## How Feelings Show Up as Aggression

We want to remind you of the three key ways children (and adults) respond to feelings: expression, suppression (and dissociation) and aggression (and agitation). Whatever feelings don't get expressed are suppressed or dissociated from and are held in the body, leading to accumulation and agitation, which in some children can then show up as aggression. Aggression happens when particular feelings have accumulated in the body, particularly fear, powerlessness and helplessness, or when a child hasn't moved all the way through the fight/flight response via expression of the feelings to a sense of relief. Aggression shows up in the following ways:

- hitting
- pushing
- taking
- throwing
- biting

Aggression is often viewed harshly in the Disconnected Domination Culture and is commonly responded to with judgement and punishment, or otherwise turning a blind eye in permissive parenting. However, from an Aware Parenting perspective, we can respond differently once we return to Aletha Solter's model of the three reasons for challenging behaviour. Remember how we talked about this earlier in the book! First is a need for information (what they understand and think). Second, their here-and-now needs (what they are needing). Third, feelings from the present or accumulated from the past (what they are feeling).

Aggression is most likely due to accumulated feelings from the past and memories of painful experiences where children went into fight mode or dissociation. (Unless something really scary happens for the child in the moment, and they go into hitting or pushing to protect themselves). Whatever percentage of feelings a child doesn't express through crying and raging accumulates in the body and can then show up as aggression (alternatively, a child can move into suppression or dissociation from the feelings).

Knowing about the accumulation of feelings can help us understand why children who hit or bite may do so suddenly, seeming relatively calm and relaxed one moment and then hitting the next. This can often be because the situation in the present is either reminding them of the past or is adding another similar feeling to the accumulation, and the cup of feelings is now at the point of overflowing.

The here-and-now experience can help them connect with similar unexpressed feelings from the past. You might have noticed this if you say no to your child, or perhaps another child tries to take something from them, and suddenly they start to hit or bite. This can be because this experience reminds them of a past painful experience where the feelings weren't fully expressed. For example, in Luana's story above, being hit in the face by the ball helped her connect with the feelings of powerlessness that had accumulated from her starting a new school.

The situations that can lead to a child feeling powerless, scared, frustrated or outraged are where they don't have agency, autonomy or choice, which are very common, particularly in the early years, and particularly in the Disconnected Domination Culture where nuclear families are the norm and we require children to do lots of things that they don't want to do. We invite you to be deeply compassionate with yourself as we go through the following list of scenarios. These experiences are common, both for our children now and probably even more so for us as children.

- Going to busy shopping areas or events.
- Being rushed to get up and go to school.
- A new sibling.
- Not having a choice in everyday events, e.g. when or what to eat.
- Daycare and other separations.
- Being left with people they don't connect with or feel safe with.
- Being put in a stroller/pushchair/buggy/car seat/highchair/playpen/ cot.
- Being told what to do.
- Experiencing power-over.
- Being taken places against their will.
- Medical interventions.
- Dentist experiences.
- Birth interventions.
- Being told that they should or have to do things.
- Learning new things that they're not able to do yet.
- Not being included in friendship groups as a tween or teen.

We can tap into the kind of feelings that they might be experiencing by thinking about times when:

- We were doing something on a computer, and it wouldn't work.
- We didn't have a choice over something important, e.g. during a lockdown.
- Other people telling us what to do.
- Not having money to pay bills.
- Our child is not doing what we ask.
- Wanting to leave the house and our child isn't willing.

Remembering these moments can help us tap into empathy for our children when they are in their equivalent moments. These feelings are really uncomfortable. Just as we don't enjoy feeling those sensations, our children don't enjoy them either. Our child doesn't want to be moving into hitting or biting. They aren't doing it deliberately. They aren't choosing to act this way. These can be REALLY helpful things to remember, particularly when they are about to pull the dog's tail.

## The Difficulty of Responding to Aggression with Compassion

To shift from the perception that a child who is hitting/biting/pushing is [*insert judgement here*] to understanding that at that moment, the child is feeling deeply painful feelings of powerlessness, fear, frustration, or outrage is a big step. Making that step, not only in how we think but also in how we feel and respond, is a huge ask. This is probably thousands of years of cultural conditioning at play here. These ways of thinking about and responding to aggression have been in many cultures for a very long time. So we invite you to be compassionate with yourself when you're finding it hard to:

- Think in compassionate ways about why our child is acting this way.
- Feel compassion and empathy, especially whilst your child is being aggressive.
- Respond with behaviour that is helpful for them.

And it's even more than our ancestral and cultural experiences. It's also about the memories stored in our bodies from our experiences. If we hit, pushed, threw or took as a child, the responses to those behaviours are stored in our bodies, feelings and consciousness. What people said about us and how they responded to us would have been taken in by us. Our feelings from how we were responded to probably were never heard. We would also have internalised how we saw the adults around us respond to other children. This is often a combination of:

- Judgement and shaming.
- Stopping the behaviour, often in a harsh or power-over way.
- Making the child apologise.
- Witholding food, love, attention, privileges, or freedom.

The above is more related to authoritarian parenting.

Or it might have been more permissive parenting by:

- Turning a blind eye to what was happening.
- Adults not moving in to stop the behaviour.
- Children being left to sort things out themselves.

Again, we invite you to have lots of compassion for yourself here. These are really common ways of responding to aggression. So, if our child hits another child or us, we are likely to experience:

- The words that we heard growing up.
- The feelings we felt as children that we couldn't express and have lovingly heard.
- The responses that we didn't get to respond with at the time.

For example, we might think, 'They are a bully,' just as we heard at school. We might feel powerless and scared, just as we did when our sibling tickled us and wouldn't stop, when a child at school was harsh to us, when our parents used power-over us or when our teacher punished us. In response, we might desire to hit back, push, or hurt when those younger parts of us and those memories show up.

And then there's simply the naturalness of the fight/flight response that can show up if we're about to be hit by our child. We can automatically switch into wanting to fight back to protect ourselves.

## Responding Effectively and Empathically to Aggression

The three causes of children's behaviour (thoughts, needs and feelings) are relevant here to us as adults. If we want our behaviour to be empathic and effective, we can also consider those three reasons.

### *What We're Thinking*

What we tell ourselves about our child's behaviour affects how we feel. If we tell ourselves there is something wrong with them, or with us, or we go into thinking about what they will become in the future, given what is happening now, we are likely to feel frustrated, scared or powerless ourselves. But we can choose to remember compassionate ways of thinking about their behaviour instead.

We invite you to refrain from any self-judgement for thinking the things that you have thought about your child/ren. You learnt these ways of thinking. You internalised these ways of thinking from your culture and family of origin. These ways of thinking have been around for hundreds of years, if not more. This is about simply being conscious of how those ways of thinking affect how you feel and behave, and increasingly choosing ways of thinking that are aligned with your values and help you be the parent you want to be.

### *What We're Needing*

In the moment, what needs do we have? What can help us be able to respond in empathic and effective ways? Do any of these resonate with you?

- **Connection:** Connecting with your breathing and the sensation of your feet on the floor (what you can see, feel and hear).
- **Power:** Reminding yourself that you are the parent, and they are the child and that you have a lot more power than them, even if it doesn't seem that way at that moment. Perhaps you'd like to get into a power pose with your feet planted on the floor, so you can feel power in your body.
- **Support:** Putting your hand on your heart to remind yourself to be compassionate with yourself and your child.

- **Protection:** Wrapping your arms around yourself, either to stop yourself from lashing out and/or to imagine yourself holding the younger or scared parts of you.
- **Presence:** Speaking phrases to yourself that help you connect with the here and now. 'I'm here with you.'
- **Compassion:** Telling your child things you want yourself to hear too, e.g. 'I see that you need some help. I'm here with you. I'm here to help. I'm here to keep everyone safe.'

## *What We're Feeling*

When our child is being aggressive, we might feel feelings of fear, shock, overwhelm, confusion, hurt or rage. These feelings might just be about the present moment. The fight/flight/freeze response means that it's normal for us to want to lash out, run away, or dissociate. Or we might try to smooth things over when these things happen. But there are also likely to be feelings from the past. Any time in the past when we experienced someone hurting us, whether that was being shouted at by our parents, being pushed by another child at school, or being hit by our sibling, those unexpressed feelings are likely to show up if we see our child hitting their sibling or pulling the dog's tail. This is how our psyche is designed to work. The feelings show up in the present to be expressed and lovingly heard. However, this is tricky when we're with our child because:

- It's not our child's job to listen to our feelings.
- Expressing those feelings to them can be scary, overwhelming and confusing for them.
- It's our job to be in the role of the parent and be there to help them.
- The feelings aren't actually in response to our child; they are in response to someone from the past.

This is why our own inner work is essential as parents. The first step is understanding that if we're feeling intense feelings when our child is doing something aggressive, those feelings are probably from the past. The second is to ask an empathic adult who is willing, to listen to those feelings and what we would love to say to our child and do. Because what we want to say is often what we would actually want to say to the person from that original experience. And/or, if we find journalling and self-inner-work effective, we can journal, listen lovingly to those feelings, and do whatever processes we do.

*The more we can express those original feelings to a loving adult listener, the less likely they will come out of our mouths to our child. Crying and raging are both part of our own healing process.*

## Responding to Aggression: Attachment Play and Loving Limits

There are two ways we can respond to aggression: attachment play and Loving Limits. In both cases, we are supporting the feelings that are coming out in aggression to come out in expression instead (remember expression, suppression, aggression!)

Since the cause of aggression is painful feelings, supporting our child to express them helps change the cause of the behaviour. Thus they are less and less likely to turn to aggression because there are fewer accumulated feelings.

### 1. *Responding to Aggression with Attachment Play*

Attachment play is a powerful way to:

- Help us feel compassionately connected with our child/ren.
- Help them experience that we are there with them, supporting them.
- Give them a sense of being loved even and especially when they are acting in this way.
- Help the feelings causing aggression to come out through laughter and body movements.

- Facilitate deeper feelings to be free to come out through crying and raging.

There's something so powerful about responding to aggression with attachment play because it goes against all that behaviour modification stands for. Behaviour modification says that when a child is doing something aggressive, we need to remove it through punishment and withdrawal of attention. The idea is that the child will fear the punishment and loss of connection and stop the behaviour. The thing about behaviour modification is that it doesn't address the source and cause of the behaviour. It simply tries to stop a child from behaving aggressively due to them feeling fear of what we will do to them if they do. (Which is likely to backfire, given that one of the main causes of aggression in the first place is unexpressed fear).

With Aware Parenting and attachment play, we respond to the source of the behaviour to create change. Instead of punishment, which creates more fear, we move in with loving warmth to help our child feel less fear and more connection. When a child is hitting, biting, or pushing, they may be feeling fear, or it might be powerlessness, frustration, outrage or overwhelm. Aware Parenting is the opposite of behaviour modification because we offer love, safety and connection. Offering these things helps children feel calmer in their bodies. Knowing that they are not alone, that we have their back, that we're with them, not against them, all these things help them feel less agitated and less in fight or flight.

We saw this in the story of Luana and her brother Felipe. When Luana was trying to control the play with the skipping rope and pulling her brother, Luana's dad used attachment play to help move the energy that was brewing within Luana. A game of tug of war was the connection needed to help Luana release some of the feelings of powerlessness.

When we remember the cause of aggression, we can see why attachment play can so often help children feel more relaxed and naturally gentle again, because they're likely to feel more connected, and they are getting to express feelings such as fear and powerlessness through play and laughter.

Laughter and play are powerful forms of healing. If you've laughed out loud watching a comedy about something relevant to you and noticed how relaxed and relieved you felt afterwards, or you've laughed loudly with a friend and then dissolved into the tears you've been waiting to cry, you'll understand why. Attachment play helps create a deep sense of connection, and works to release fear and powerlessness through laughter, which can be the source of aggression. Attachment play helps loosen up deeper and bigger feelings that can then bubble out through raging and crying.

*Types of Attachment Play:*

Generally, the most apt form of attachment play to help at the time of the aggression is power-reversal games. We play the less powerful, less able, less competent one, and we support our child in feeling exaggeratedly more powerful, more able and more competent.

One of the simplest power-reversal games is a pillow fight. If your child is about to hit you or has hit, you can offer to play this with them. Only in the game you exaggeratedly fall over each time our child hits you with the pillow; being mock surprised that they keep on knocking you over can also really help. You might find that after you do this a few times, your child asks for a pillow fight when the feelings are bubbling up which might have led to hitting.

Another power-reversal game is a scary chase game – with your child chasing you. So, you might start with something like, 'Whatever you do, don't chase me!' in a silly or goofy voice. But in this chasing game, you keep pretending to fall over or being surprised when they catch you.

*If they're laughing, and there's no tickling[6], then they are releasing the feelings that are causing the aggression.*

6. We'll explain about why not to tickle on page 140.

Marion reminisces:

> A game that I made up when my son was hitting and head-butting after his father and I split up is the Shall We Dance? Game. I found this one helpful because I sang the song, 'Shall we dance!?' (Remember the musical, The King and I?) This helped me stay really warm and loving and calm whilst my son was still trying to hit me. As he went to hit, I would catch his hand, pretend to do different dances, such as the tango, and say something silly like, 'Oh, we're doing the Tango now, are we?' and then sing the song. I kept on going as he tried to hit and lash out, naming different dances, and we would end up laughing and connected.

Now you understand the principles of attachment play, we invite you to remember this process to stop your child from being aggressive through attachment play.

- Pause to understand the cause of the behaviour.
- Move close to your child with love, warmth, and playfulness.
- Offer to play a game in which they have power-over you. In time, you will probably find yourself and your child making up your own games. Pillow fights where they knock you over, chasing games where they catch you and push-you-off-the bed games where they push you over, all help release powerlessness and create a sense of power, particularly if we mock surprise each time they do it.
- Help them express and release feelings of fear, powerlessness and frustration through laughter.
- Be ready to listen if deeper feelings emerge and your child is ready to express them through crying or raging.

Aware Parenting is based on the understanding that children know exactly what they need to heal – and that includes knowing exactly which attachment play will help that healing. We invite you to see attachment play as a loving experiment. We never really know exactly what will support a child to feel more connected and to express the feelings causing the aggression. One game might help a child one time and not another. One game might help one child and not another child. Most important is our willingness to play and discover together what helps our child at those moments. There is no right or wrong here.

Your child might not move into connection and laughter. That's one of the reasons it's helpful to know that there is another option – Loving Limits.

## 2. Responding to Aggression with Loving Limits

Loving Limits are based on the understanding that we say a loving no to the behaviour and a loving yes to the feelings that are causing the behaviour. We are stopping the aggression, knowing that the cause is powerlessness, fear, frustration or outrage, and supporting our child's feelings to be expressed, released and heard.

As we saw in Luana's story when her dad offered a Loving Limit on the trampoline, he said no to the hitting and yes to the feelings caused by Luana's school experiences. We are more likely to be able to offer effective Loving Limits if we are feeling relatively calm and centred. Attending to that list of three causes (thoughts, needs, and feelings) is important, so that might mean:

1. Telling ourselves compassionate things about our child and ourselves.
2. Meeting our needs in that moment to stay centred and calm.
3. Attending to our feelings on an ongoing basis, so they're less likely to explode out at moments like this.

We invite you to connect with your own personalised version of this by writing down your answers to the following questions (and keeping them somewhere you will see them often) so you're ready for this scenario if it occurs:

1. What key phrases could you say to yourself when your child is aggressive or heading that way?
2. What would you like to do to help yourself stay calm and centred in a deeply embodied way?

3. What would help the younger parts of you know that you are safe and powerful in those moments?

If your child often shows aggression, you might want to connect with those things frequently. For example, when you're in the shower, you might imagine yourself in that calm state, offering a Loving Limit to your child, thinking those thoughts, meeting those needs, and communicating to those younger parts that you are safe and powerful. And of course, the more concise this is, the easier it will be – so although at first, this might seem a lot, once you've practised it, you will probably find becoming more and more second nature.

## Expressing a Loving Limit

Remember, **we're saying no to the aggression and yes to the expression underneath**. This means that when we offer a Loving Limit, we're not expecting them to say, 'Okay' and then feel calm. So, when we stop the behaviour, we want and expect the feelings to come out instead.

With a Loving Limit, we come in with the minimum limit required. If there is vocal aggression from the child, we might just express a verbal Loving Limit. If the aggression is physical, we will likely need to offer a physical Loving Limit.

If our child is about to throw something, we might put out our hand to hold the object and prevent the throwing but not take it (unless we can't keep everyone safe by simply holding the object). If they are about to hit someone, we might put out our hand to hold their arm or hand to prevent the hitting. If they are about to bite, we might need to put our hand on their forehead or chin to stop the biting. If they're about to push, we might need to get in between them and the other person. We might also do other things to keep them and ourselves safe, such as putting a pillow between them and us if they're hitting or kicking on the floor.

If they've already started hitting, pushing, biting or taking, and it's continuing, the invitation is for us to get in and prevent more from happening. If the hitting has already happened and stopped, that's where we might need to move in with attachment play (see above).

When we step in with the Loving Limit, our child might respond by continuing to hit or bite or push or take. At this point, we want to remind you that what you're telling yourself will have a big impact. If you're making judgements about them or yourself, you're liable to feel frustrated or powerless. So, you might want to remind yourself that your child is behaving like this because they're upset, AND they need your help to let the underlying feelings out. We might need to repeat the Loving Limit over and over. This is part of connecting to the feelings. So, the words we might use[7] might be something like, 'I'm not willing for you to hit Mark, and I'm right here, sweetheart, and I'm listening. I'm not willing for you to do that.' Or your word might simply be 'No', with a loving quality to it.

With aggression, because we want to stop the behaviour, we are most likely to express the limit first: 'I'm not willing for you to [*name the behaviour*].' And then the love, which expresses through our tone, expression, and movements, as well as the specific words that we are expressing: '... and I'm right here, and I'm listening.' So, in our words, we are expressing no to the behaviour: 'I'm not willing for you to [*name the behaviour*]' – And the yes to the feelings: '... and I'm right here, and I'm listening.

The love comes from the tone of your voice, adding the endearments like 'sweetheart', 'darling', as well as phrases like, 'I'm here,' I'm listening,' 'I see that you're upset,' 'I love you,' 'I'm here to help,' 'I'm here to keep everyone safe.' Perhaps you might like to think how you would feel if someone said each of the phrases to you and whether you feel a different quality and response.

## Loving Limits Language

When offering a Loving Limit, we use language that creates a connection. This is because, for a Loving Limit to help a child move from aggression to expression, they need to feel a sense of connection with us.

'I-statements' are most helpful because they are more likely to create a connection with us. e.g. 'I'm not willing for you to hit Johnny, and I'm here, and I'm listening, and I love you.' Also, avoiding judgement, shame or blame, e.g. 'I'm not willing for you to [*name the behaviour*].' rather than, 'it's not okay to hit!' When we express the Loving Limit in ways that create connection and offer loving compassion, this is most likely to support our child to feel the loving support and move from the aggression to the expression.

Less helpful language doesn't create a connection or might lead to shame or guilt. For example, we don't recommend 'It's not okay to hit' or 'That's not okay' because we're not using an 'I' statement, so there isn't a connection, and the 'not okay' is a judgement, so our child is less likely to feel connected and more likely to experience being judged, and whatever feelings are bubbling inside are likely to increase.

Also, we suggest avoiding unclear or inaccurate language, such as, 'We don't hit in this family.' (Because they just have!) And if they have hit, does that mean they don't belong in the family? That can be scary for a child. We also don't recommend 'be gentle' because they can't think themselves out of those feelings. It doesn't address how they're feeling or help them release the feelings that are the true cause of the behaviour.

So, the language of Loving Limits expresses our loving understanding and compassion and our clear capacity to stop the behaviour. We can aim to match that with what we are expressing in our tone and our body language – that we are feeling calm and loving, and we are there to keep everyone safe. This can thus elicit the kind of connection and safety to support the expression of feelings.

When we offer a Loving Limit, our child might try to continue with the aggression, in which case, we can keep expressing the Loving Limit whilst keeping close. They may also start to tussle, wriggle, or avoid connection, and our response can be to stay close, still with empathy and the Loving Limit. Or they might move into the big expression of feelings with tears and/or tantrums, and we can listen lovingly.

If our child is frustrated, angry or outraged, it can be really important to meet the intensity of their feelings by matching their tone. For some children, if they are really in the big feelings, and we meet it with a calm voice, they may experience that we don't really understand or empathise with how intensely they are feeling those feelings. So, saying, 'I REALLY HEAR HOW FRUSTRATED YOU ARE,'[8] with deep compassion can give them a sense of being deeply heard and understood, without joining them in their big feelings.

If the Loving Limit stops the behaviour, but no expression comes out, we suggest you stay close and stay loving. The feelings that bubbled up in the hitting are still there, and if they don't let them out, they will still be there, ready to come out at another time. We invite you to keep an eye out, knowing those feelings are close to the surface and be ready to step in again and ideally prevent anyone from getting hurt. You also might want to move to attachment play if the Loving Limit doesn't seem to be helping any expression.

## Helping Your Child Express Their Feelings

If there's lots of aggression and you don't seem to be helping your child express those feelings either through Loving Limits or attachment play, there can be a few things you can do to help in general, including:

- Increase the amount of non-directive child-centred play, where you offer them your undivided attention and follow their lead, within an environment where they have plenty of things to choose to play with.

- Increase the amount of power-reversal games you're playing – where you play the less powerful role and be mock-surprised that they are stronger than you.

- More inner work for you including what you're telling yourself, how to meet your needs in the moment of aggression, and your own childhood memories and feelings, with some loving listening!

Sometimes children won't move into expressing big feelings as they sense that the parent or caregiver aren't able to be present with those feelings. It's always helpful to check in with your willingness to really be with the feelings that may surface. We also invite you to keep practising! We found that Loving Limits took a lot of practice to really embody!

### *Attachment Play or Loving Limit – How to Choose*

This is an experiment and will be different for each child. Often, it will depend on how you are feeling and your emotional spaciousness. Do you have the energy to move in with attachment play? We invite you to follow that. Are you in a calm and centred enough place to offer a Loving Limit and listen to crying or raging? If so, we invite you to do that.

You might also sense that the most helpful response depends on the accumulated feelings and the situation. For example, you might find that attachment play is more helpful if you can see the feelings bubbling up, but there's no aggression happening (yet). Whereas you might find that a Loving Limit is being called for if your child already seems to be feeling a lot of feelings alongside the aggression.

If you've been expressing Loving Limits and no expression has been happening, you might go for attachment play. If you have a sense that your child really needs to have a big cry with you, you might go for Loving Limits.

## Reducing Aggression and Its Causes

There are a few key things we can do to reduce aggression from happening in the first place. We can reduce its causes in children by:

- Giving choices wherever possible (e.g. which pyjamas, which toothpaste, which book).
- Honouring their no wherever possible.
- Avoiding using power-over, 'should' and 'have-to'.

- Avoiding punishment, shaming or blaming.
- Supporting agency wherever possible (e.g. if they can do something themselves and enjoy doing it, supporting them in doing it rather than doing it for them).
- Offering empathy when they feel frustrated, 'I hear that you feel frustrated, sweetheart.'
- Offering regular non-directive child-centred play, where you follow their lead and give them your undivided attention.
- Providing opportunities for power-reversal games such as pillow fights and Lawrence Cohen's swing game (you pretend that they are knocking you over each time they swing forward, and they laugh a lot!).
- Offering attachment play to support their cooperation with daily activities like toothbrushing.

CHAPTER 7

# Fear, Anxiety, Trust, Attachment and Separation

Lael shares with us:

*Brigette had come for a session with me to explore whether going to preschool was the right fit for her daughter. In the questionnaire she completed and sent before our session, she shared that her daughter Nova cried at drop-off and Brigette was feeling very worried about it. She shared how she had tried different things, such as asking her partner to drop off Nova, such as using rewards if she said goodbye without crying, but nothing had worked. Now every morning, the first thing Nova said was, 'Is it a kinder day today?'*

*The first thing I asked Brigette was whether she thought preschool was a helpful place for Nova. Brigette shared, 'It's a sweet little centre. The staff are kind, and there are only fifteen kids, and when Nova stayed, she enjoyed it. It's just saying goodbye. She clings to me and screams, and I can't handle it. Even though the staff don't push me to do anything, my heart breaks, and I feel like bursting into tears.'*

*I offer Brigette lots of empathy. There is no doubt that witnessing our children in situations like hers is painful, and it can bring up a lot of feelings for us. As we move deeper into Brigette's story, she shares that when Nova was eighteen months old, she had to go away for two weeks for work. Nova was with her dad for those two weeks, but Brigette still carries a great deal of guilt for leaving her. 'I swear she was different from that moment on. When I returned, she would freak out if I left the room just to go to the toilet. She wanted me all the time, would often* refuse to go to her dad, and now I can't leave her anywhere. I keep telling myself she will grow out of it, but it's getting worse.'

I ask Brigette to tell me more about the guilt.

She explains that she thinks it's her fault and that she shouldn't have gone away, 'Every time I take her to preschool, that same guilt surfaces, and I think to myself, I'm doing it to her all over again.' On some level, Brigette is accurate.

The same feelings are surfacing for both of them each time a drop-off occurs. The separation that Nova is experiencing brings up similar feelings to those she probably felt when Brigette left for work.

Brigette shared that her partner did a wonderful job taking care of Nova when she was away, and she was kept busy, so she didn't have time to miss her mum, so it was only when Brigette returned that they began to see any big reactions from Nova. From an Aware Parenting perspective, if a child doesn't have the opportunity to express big feelings in relation to separation, often they will surface again in situations that are similar to the initial incident. Nova's expression of fear and tears at separation may be the feelings that were present when Brigette went away for work. When we understand that children know what to do to release these feelings, we can see that Nova brings the repressed feelings to the surface each time separation is imminent.

I ask Brigette what it would be like if she supported Nova to express her fears and worries about saying goodbye in a safe way. Brigette shared that she could see how that would help, but she doesn't think she has it in her to hold it.

'It just makes me want to cry.' I lean in closer to Brigette and ask her to tell me all about her feelings. I invite her to say all the things she wished *she could say about this situation, and I let her know that her tears are welcome.*

*Brigette looks tentative, but she starts with how frustrated she is by how long this has been going on. She then moves into how she feels guilty for the decision she made two years ago. She also vents about how she just wishes her daughter could say goodbye and go off and play like all the other kids.*

*As Brigette gets in touch with her feelings, she quietly sobs that she believes she has damaged her daughter. She shares her worries about what will happen in the future. I welcome all of Brigette's feelings. For twenty minutes, she cries and expresses all she has been holding onto. When she feels calm again, I ask her the same question I asked her earlier. 'Do you think it is safe for Nova to go to preschool?'*

*After a big pause, she says, 'Yes, it's safe for her to go. I just have been sending her the message that it's not. My fears, my guilt, that's what I've been showing her. No wonder she doesn't want to go.'*

*We begin to discuss some ideas to support Nova in releasing the feelings that have been trying to come out. We discuss playing games and more opportunities to hold space for feelings related to separation. Brigette begins to see there are so many things she and her partner can do to help Nova's feelings related to separation without even leaving the house. By the end of our session, Brigette feels so much calmer thinking about preschool.*

## Thoughts, Needs and Feelings

In Brigette's story, we can see that Nova's fear can be connected to thoughts and understanding, choice and autonomy, and present and past feelings. Do you recognise that same list of three again?

### 1. *Thoughts and Understanding*

Nova may need more information about what happens on a preschool day and more explanation about the drop-off process. For example, 'I will sit with you in the car before you go in and listen to any feelings you want to tell me. When we arrive, I can come in and read a book with you or play something you would like to play and then we can say goodbye at the door. If you have big feelings, I will stay to listen or your teacher will listen later. Then I will be back to pick you up in four hours.' The older the child, the more likely it is that thoughts will be affecting their feeling state. Giving children clear information can help them be less likely to feel fear in the first place.

### 2. *Needs for Choice and Autonomy*

Nova isn't choosing to go to preschool, so her anxiety may show about her lack of autonomy and choice about what happens throughout her day. (This is a common theme for children, particularly in our current education system that still promotes separation of children from their parents, coercion and behaviour modification.) Children can be particularly likely to feel fear if they are experiencing a lot of things that they haven't had a choice about. A new sibling, going to the dentist, being coerced into doing things. The more choices we can give children, the less likely they are to feel scared.

### 3. *Feelings in the Here and Now or From Past Stress or Trauma Showing Up*

Brigette's instincts were telling her that many of Nova's fears were connected to an earlier separation and her unexpressed feelings from the past. The more a child has unexpressed feelings from the past, the more likely they will be scared about new things in the present and future.

## Establishing Trust

As we can see in Brigette's story, when children are experiencing challenges, this is often an invitation for us to explore our own beliefs and childhood experiences. Children highlight the parts of our past that need healing or attention. When we work with parents who bring an issue with their child, we often invite them to look at their own earlier experiences. If a parent can be present with their child in whatever situation is challenging, information and practices can help them support their child. However, if the parent finds holding the space for their child's upset hard, or they are quick to feel anger, or the situation isn't shifting despite them offering apt support, there is usually an invitation to some healing of their own past.

If we can trust that our children know what they need to do to find their way back into a balanced state, our role becomes about creating safe spaces and opportunities for them to do so. However, trusting that our children know what they need to do to heal their past hurts can be challenging for many of us.

Can we trust that our children are perfect just the way they are? Can we trust our intuition to guide us? Can we trust that life is taking care of us? Can we trust ourselves as parents? So much of Aware Parenting holds space for feelings, but if we find trust hard, we may find it difficult to be present with the expression of big emotions.

If you were to reflect on the messages you received about trust from your parents or caregivers, did you hear your parents say, 'You can't trust anyone'? Did you pick up on infidelity in your family, which meant you couldn't trust a parent? Did you believe that you couldn't trust yourself if your parents often told you that you were 'being silly', or, 'don't be scared'? Exploring trust can help us make sense of why we find it hard to trust life and our child/ren's journey.

Over decades of working with families, we have no doubt that children innately know what they need to do to heal from stress and trauma and connect to their state of calm presence. They need a loving, supportive and emotionally safe environment and the trust that they know what they are doing.

## *Children who are scared often have an accumulation of past feelings that show up as being frightened of the future.*

This applies to all of us, not just children. If we didn't get to express our feelings from experiences we had in the past to a loving listener – whether that is an experience at school, as a tween, or an incident at work as an adult – we can feel fear, and will tend to imagine similar possible scenarios that may happen in the future. As we have explored previously – our willingness to feel and express the full array of emotions supports us to journey through life with more openness and real courage, with compassion and true resilience. Trusting our child's journey as they travel through the more challenging parts of life and trusting our ability to be with them in the ways they need is a gift that helps our child develop a deep belief in themselves to meet life with all it has to offer. This is true resilience.

If your child does feel anxiety or has big fears, then using the following games can be of great benefit.

### *Separation Games*

These are one of the nine varieties of attachment play that Aletha Solter developed.

Separation games are all about releasing feelings of fear and worry that exist related to separation. The key to healing is providing enough connection so that our child knows we are still there with them, but with small experiences of separation. The loss must be the accurate length of time so that it doesn't become scary for them.

Separation games are helpful for children who feel scared or upset in relation to separation and those who experience regular separations. They also help healing happen from past painful separations or fears around separation that happen after losses in the family.

- **Adapted peek-a-boo** with young children. You can put an object (such as a teddy or pillow) between you for a moment and then pretend that you don't know where they have gone. Again, you can show great surprise when you see them again!
- **Where are you?** Have your child sit on your lap, and when they look away, look around the room, saying, 'Where's Johnny? When they look back again, make eye contact and show great surprise, 'Ahh, THERE you are!' Wait for them to look away again and repeat. This is a glorious game because it gives the child choices about when to connect and disconnect, which can help bring healing and a sense of power when there have been previous separations that they didn't choose.
- **Hide and seek:** Again, you know this one well! If it is a younger child, ensure that another person hides with them – either a sibling or an adult. Show great surprise and jump up in the air when you are found! Again, this can still be played with older children.
- **Don't leave me game:** When they go to leave or cross the room, you gently grab hold of their clothes and beg them not to leave you. Let them drag you across the floor if they are big enough – while you mock beg.
- **Love notes game:** This is for an older child or teen who has barricaded themselves in their room. Slip love notes under their door (pictures if they are not yet reading) and beg and plead in a funny way for her to come out. (Thank you to Lawrence Cohen of Playful Parenting for this game!)

## Contingency Games

These are another kind of attachment play and are games where our child has a sense of agency. In these games, the actions the child takes affect the world; our behaviour is repeatedly contingent upon our child's behaviour. They give children power and choice, counteracting and healing feelings of powerlessness and fear. These games can be helpful for fears such as being scared of monsters at night. Here are a few examples:

- **Magic wand game:** They get to choose what happens when they direct the wand at you and you do what they ask, often in big or exaggerated ways.
- **Piggyback game:** They ride on your back, and they get to choose where you go.
- **Tummy poke game:** When they poke your tummy, you make a funny noise, smile, or do something funny.
- **Teddy touch game:** They drop a toy, such as a teddy, and you say 'ouch!'
- **Simon says:** Where you do what the child says. This works well with older children.

Attachment play will often help children release lighter fears and more surface feelings. However, the more fear or anxiety, the more likely the child will also need to express feelings through crying to release those feelings. Crying, shaking and trembling are other powerful release and relaxation processes that support the release of stress hormones and tension in the body after frightening events. Children's bodies are so wise! You might want to refer back to Chapter 3 on crying to recap.

**CHAPTER 8**

# Sleep

*Pippa and Stacey were walking their eighteen-month-old boys around the park. They were trying to get their little ones to sleep as it was 'nap time', and as they always joked to each other, 'our boys just hate to sleep!'*

*'I swear I nearly walked for two hours the other day trying to get Max to sleep; he just fought it the whole time,' shared Pippa.*

*'I hear you on that,' said Stacey. 'Dom took ninety minutes to fall asleep for his daytime nap last week, and I breastfed him about thirty times that night!'*

*Both mothers value connection and attachment for their boys. Since birth, they've done everything they could to meet their babies' needs. From the beginning, Pippa and Stacey bonded in their mothers' group as they both loved gentle parenting techniques. They often got together to talk about their ups and downs of mothering and share tips and ideas they'd come across. After 18 months of very frequent night waking and toddlers that didn't seem that happy, both mothers were exhausted in trying to meet their sons' apparent needs. 'I didn't think it would be this hard,' said Pippa, that lunchtime.*

*Sleep was an issue for the boys, and both mothers did everything they could to get them to go to sleep. They were often breastfeeding all through the night, and even though both mothers really valued breastfeeding, they often discussed weaning in the hope that Max and Dom would sleep better. Stacey was even considering going away for the weekend and leaving Max with his dad, as another friend had done with her toddler, just to get the weaning over and done with. Neither mother*

> *wanted to stop breastfeeding, but the exhaustion was getting to breaking point and weaning seemed the only option.*

Pippa's and Stacey's experience is one that we have both come across many times. Beautiful, attuned mothers who value closeness, attachment, bonding and breastfeeding but who are finding that their toddlers are waking up more and more as they get older, rather than less.

## Sleep Theory

Regarding sleep, parents often think there are only two main choices. Either choosing attachment and needing to put up with broken sleep and early mornings for several years; or having restful sleep and giving up on attachment and closeness. Have you ever thought that you only have those two choices? Aware Parenting offers a third way.

Instead of needing to choose between sleep OR connection, attunement and attachment, Aware Parenting shows us that we can have both. When we understand the three things babies and children need for restful sleep and we cooperate with their natural and inbuilt relaxation processes, we don't need to experience years of broken nights and early mornings or sacrifice closeness and responsiveness to our children. In this chapter, we'll explain more. Oh, and even though we are talking about babies and younger children here, the same principles apply to tweens and teens (and adults too!)

Aware Parenting has a very different understanding of sleep compared to most other parenting approaches, and these differences lead to really different practices. In many other approaches, you might hear:

- Babies and children fight or resist sleep.
- They don't want to sleep.
- They need to be taught to sleep.

- They need to learn how to sleep.
- They need us to do lots of things to them to make them sleep.
- Or they need us to leave them alone for them to learn to sleep.

From an Aware Parenting perspective, we have very different ways of understanding why babies and children often won't go to sleep when they are tired. And, if you think about this from a wider historical perspective of human beings, does it make sense that babies and children would fight sleep or need to be taught to do it? Sleep is a vital physiological need – which is why depriving people of sleep is a form of torture. Our bodies desperately need it!

If you think about all the other ways that children's bodies are primed to flourish, does the whole 'fighting sleep' perception make sense? Think of how a baby's body and mother's body are finely intertwined and work together with exquisite harmony during pregnancy and birth. Or breastfeeding, when the amount and kind of suckling profoundly affects the type and amount of milk a mother produces. Does it make sense to think that babies and children would be so incapable of sleeping, which is such a fundamental physiological human need?

But if sleep is natural, why do so many babies and children not sleep as much as their bodies need? Why do many babies and children not go to sleep when they are tired? Why does it appear that they don't want to sleep? Why do many babies and children often wake up before they've had enough sleep, often with increasing frequency as they get older, even though their stomachs are bigger and can hold more? What's going on?

We find it helpful to ask parents to reflect on their own experiences to see if that brings clarity and understanding, and we invite you to do that.

Do you remember times when you felt really tired, but took hours to go to sleep? Can you recall waking up in the middle of the night and taking ages to get back to sleep? What about waking up really early, still tired, and not being able to get back to sleep? If so, were those times when you were thinking about something that happened that day where you felt uncomfortable? Perhaps there were things you didn't say or didn't express to another person that you wanted to say? Or perhaps you felt overwhelmed after a really busy day and even though you were really tired, you could feel all the overwhelm swirling around and you weren't able to go to sleep? Or perhaps you've woken up in the middle of the night feeling anxious or sad or agitated, or just with a general sense of unease?

What about when you sleep really soundly and restfully? What kinds of things have happened before that? Were you feeling really happy? Did you have lots of connection and laughter? Perhaps you experienced intimacy with your partner? Or maybe you expressed some big feelings to someone who was listening to you, and you felt really relieved after letting it out? For one reason or another, were you feeling really relaxed in your body?

Babies and children can also find it hard to go to sleep and stay asleep when:

- They've had an overwhelming day and haven't released the stress from it. (Remember, babies and small children can be easily overwhelmed by things that are everyday occurrences for us!)
- They haven't had the chance to express their feelings about things that happened.
- They're feeling sad, confused, scared, frustrated or agitated.
- Something stressful happened to them and the feelings, physical tension and stress hormones from the fight or flight response are still weighing heavy in their body.

Of course, there may be physical things, too – so please always consider these first. This can include allergies, food intolerance, teething or sickness, or responses to external things like chemicals in food, bedding, cleaning products, soaps, and also electromagnetic radiation and other environmental factors such as loud noises.

Otherwise, babies and children can sleep more soundly and restfully when:

- They've had plenty of physical closeness and contact.

- They've laughed and played with us.
- They've expressed their feelings to us, and we've listened.
- They feel relaxed and relatively free from tension.

So, from an Aware Parenting perspective, babies and children need three things to sleep restfully and soundly.[9] (This applies to adults too!):

1. To feel tired.
2. To feel connected.
3. To feel relaxed.

## 1. Feeling Tired

We know that this seems obvious, but it's really important to keep tiredness in mind. Have you ever gone to bed really early, perhaps because you're getting up early in the morning to go on holiday, and you're not tired, and you find it hard to go to sleep?

We can watch for cues of tiredness in our baby or child and might observe such things as yawning, eyes drooping, rubbing their eyes, a lack of coordination, or wanting to lie down.

However, some of the things that other parenting paradigms see as signs of tiredness – being 'silly', running around, being loud, rambunctious, crying, tantrums, being agitated, indicate something different from an Aware Parenting perspective.

From an Aware Parenting lens, when babies, children and adults are tired, we are less able to suppress our feelings. *We're designed that way – to let out the feelings before we sleep so that our bodies feel more relaxed.* Remember we talked about the natural homeostatic processes of the body, to return to a state of calm after overwhelming, stressful or traumatic events? This is part of that. Many of those things in the list above aren't a sign of tiredness. They are an indication that feelings are trying to surface to be released as part of our natural relaxation

9. This is a model that Marion created based on Aletha's work.

processes, designed to help restful sleep and through that, overall health and wellbeing. We will discuss more about this in the relaxation section.

## 2. Feeling Connected

When a child goes to sleep, there is a letting go of daytime consciousness and a sinking into a different state. Thinking about what an amazing process that is and how a child might feel when they are on the cusp of going to sleep can help us step into their shoes and understand what they might be experiencing.

The more connected a child feels before sleep and whilst going to sleep, the easier it is for them to relax into sleep. The connection they feel in their body signals to their nervous system that it's safe to sleep. We can see this has a survival function – a baby or child who senses they are alone doesn't know that they are safe, and so staying awake is likely to be safer – since they can then move into fight, flight or freeze if danger comes.

Connection signals safety. The younger they are, the more they will need that connection whilst they are going to sleep to experience a sense of safety. As children get older, they can internalise that sense of connection from their experiences during the day and evening. They also have the cognitive understanding that adults are close, so they are safe to go to sleep even if they are alone. However, older children will still need to feel a sense of connection sometime during the day and particularly leading up to sleep. This means that the more connected and present we are with ourselves, and the more we offer them that closeness and warmth, the more they will feel that connection and carry it with them into their sleep.

How do babies and young children go to sleep if they don't feel connected? Often they will need to suppress or dissociate from feelings related to not having closeness, and they might do things to make that happen, such as sucking their thumb or fingers, clutching on to a blanket or soft toy, getting into a particular position every time, or using repetitive movements. Or we might do things to them, like jiggling or rocking them, bouncing them, feeding them, or giving them a dummy. These all help them dissociate from any feelings of aloneness, fear or tension enough for them to go to sleep. These feelings often bubble up again when they move into a lighter sleep. They may then wake up again after one or more sleep cycles, after which they will either call out or repeat whatever it was they did to suppress the feelings the first time. Again, if you see your baby or child doing that, please put down those emotional sticks, as Marion calls them. Judging yourself or feeling guilty is a form of punishment that doesn't actually help you or them. Self-compassion is key here!

## 3. Feeling Relaxed

This is where Aware Parenting differs from most other parenting modalities. Remember when we talked about those times when we might find it hard to go to sleep, or we might wake up at night or early in the morning when we've got feelings bubbling and are thinking about events from the past? We're not feeling relaxed at those times, and it's really hard to go to sleep without feeling relaxed.

To go to sleep, a child (all ages of people, actually, but we're going to talk about children here!) needs to feel relaxed in their body. To go from being awake to being asleep, we need to feel sufficiently relaxed. In other parenting paradigms, there is the belief that we need to do things to babies or children to make them relaxed. For example, we might:

- Feed them.
- Rock or jiggle them.
- Sing to them.
- Take them for a drive in the car.
- Push them in a stroller.
- Read to them.
- Ask them to read to themselves.
- Give them a dummy or pacifier.

All these things are often working against a child's inbuilt ability to move towards relaxation. As Marion often says, 'they're not fighting sleep, we're fighting their natural relaxation processes.'

Again, we would love to invite you to reflect on those times when you're feeling overwhelmed or agitated or sad, or you're ruminating on something that you didn't say to someone that day. You might find yourself doing the adult versions of working against your natural relaxation process. That might be having a glass or two of wine, having just one more snack, watching Netflix, scrolling social media, looking at TikTok videos or reading a book. Do you find that sometimes when you do these things, once you turn off the light, you still feel agitated, or you wake up in the middle of the night?

Often, we are just bypassing our feelings. We aren't listening to them. We're simply distracting ourselves or dissociating. Those feelings are still there, which might mean that we're restless, keep waking up, or we wake up and can't get to sleep for hours. The same often happens to babies and children. We might do all these things to try to make them feel relaxed, but this isn't a deep relaxation. It's more superficial because the true cause of their lack of relaxation isn't being addressed and those feelings are still sitting in their bodies. The agitation, the tension, and the stress hormones mean they are still on alert, making it hard for them to feel relaxed enough to sleep or if they do go to sleep, they might wake up next sleep cycle or when there is a noise. This is where, without this information, parents might think their child is 'fighting sleep' when really, they would love to be feeling truly and deeply relaxed so that they can go to sleep!

And again, of course, there can be physiological reasons here – reactions to food, or the chemicals in bedding, or electromagnetic radiation and so on, so please always keep in mind the physical as well as the emotional reasons!

## Helping Our Children Sleep Restfully

To help out child/ren feel relaxed and sleep soundly, we need to address the root causes:

- Watch for their tiredness cues and respond in an attuned way.
- Help them feel connected.
- Cooperate with their natural relaxation processes.

### 1. Noticing Tiredness Cues

We can watch out for tiredness cues and respond promptly if possible (by offering them closeness and an opportunity to express feelings through play and laughter or crying and raging, which we talk about below). We can remember that crying and rambunctious playing aren't signs that tiredness is painful, rather, they are actually our children trying to use their natural relaxation processes.

### 2. Helping Them Feel More Connected

For children, cuddles, closeness and rough and tumble bring a deep sense of connection. We invite you to follow your child's lead here. Clearly, if they're already relaxed in bed, you won't be inviting vigorous play. But if they are inviting you to play rough and tumble type games, then joining in can help them feel deeply connected!

In contrast, if your child is wriggling around, pinching your skin or repeatedly kicking off their covers, cuddling them will not bring true relaxation, because those things are likely to be symptoms of accumulated feelings.

Relaxed physical closeness signals to a child's nervous system that they are safe to sleep. If you're saying, 'I DO offer lots of closeness, and they still won't go to sleep!' There are a few things to consider:

The more present we are, the more the child feels our presence. Often at the end of the day, we might not be present at all. We might be desperate to have some time to do something else. We might feel frustrated, resentful, stressed, or agitated – and our children really feel that. (We're sending so much love to you every time you're in that position. We know how hard that can be!)

So, one of the things that can support them is to help ourselves. That might be having a bath together. It might be pausing for a few moments doing some yoga or meditation or self-empathy whilst they are doing something else. Another option is to get in and do some rough and tumble play, especially before they go into a more relaxed mode. Physical play where there's lots of body contact can often help us feel more relaxed so that our children feel really connected with us.

Sometimes cuddles are enough to give them that deep sense of connection, but often, a more high-energy connection is needed, especially if they are inviting physical play – which is the subject of our next point:

## 3. *Helping Them Feel More Relaxed*

The first thing to address is physical needs. This rules out things like too much light or noise, uncomfortable pyjamas or bed linen. Creating a physically relaxing environment can be a part of this – comfortable nightwear and linen in natural fibres, dim lighting, and a relaxed ambience. Reading stories and singing songs might help them feel relaxed, but they can just as easily work against their own natural relaxation processes.

## Natural Relaxation Processes

If our child is agitated, and we try to make them feel relaxed with stories and songs, we can sometimes distract them from their bodies. We are bypassing the feelings. The agitation stays there in their body and makes it hard for them to sleep, or they wake up again when the sensations and feelings bubble up.

Whereas, if we work with their natural relaxation processes, going with them, trusting that their body knows what to do, the agitation gets released from their body, and they can fall asleep, feeling truly relaxed. This means they sleep and stay asleep until their body has had enough sleep or they are truly hungry.

These processes help our child release the agitation from their body. There are three main ways that this process works.

1. Talking with loving support.
2. Play and laughter with loving support.
3. Crying, raging and tantrums with loving support.

## 1. *Talking with Loving Support*

Your child may share about their day or discuss a worry they have. Sometimes they might ask you questions. At times like this, offering a gentle listening ear can be so beneficial, not giving advice unless they ask us for it. The younger the child, the more the release needs to be physical and physiological, through laughter and play or crying and raging with physical movement. Talking is less effective with younger children if they have feelings or any agitation on board.

With tweens and teens, brain development can also affect how and when they go to sleep. Normal adolescent sleep patterns are different from those of children and adults. Melatonin (the sleep hormone) levels in the blood naturally rise later at night and fall later in the morning in teens compared to most children and adults. The growing brain of a teen can mean that the prefrontal cortex shuts off in the evening (so doing homework late at night isn't so helpful), and the amygdala (the emotional centre of the brain) becomes more active. It's why teens will often want to discuss what's going on in their world at 10 p.m. Many teens can need this connection time to share their thoughts and worries so that they can sleep.

*Teens need deep listening without judgement, advice or panic in response to what they share. If you can listen with empathy and not offer advice unless requested, this can create even greater trust with your teen.*

## 2. Play and Laughter (Attachment Play) with Loving Support

Laughter and particular kinds of play are highly therapeutic and help children process events and release feelings. Attachment play also helps create feelings of deep connection. Remember that feeling connected is one of the things they need to sleep peacefully, so this kind of play works on two of the levels – connection and relaxation.

If they're being silly and goofy, we can join in and play with them, and if there's laughter happening, then they are expressing feelings from their day. We do not recommend tickling, even if a child asks for it, because it is too stimulating on a sensory level. Perhaps you remember being tickled by an older sibling or bigger peer and laughing but feeling overwhelmed and powerless? Play particularly releases feelings like fear and powerlessness and feelings related to not yet being able to do things, which are all really common for children to feel. When a child releases those feelings from their bodies through laughing and playing with us, they feel more truly relaxed.

Have you ever laughed a lot with friends and then felt so relaxed in your body and gone to sleep really easily that night? When we join in with their play and laughter, we might often feel much more connected and relaxed too! This can also help our sleep!

What we tell ourselves is so important here! If we have judgments about why they are doing it, we are likely to feel frustrated and agitated. Whereas if we're reminding ourselves that it's their natural relaxation process and they're doing this to feel more relaxed and to sleep more easily, we're more likely to feel compassionate and connected and willing to join in.

Lael says:

> 'My daughter Tali was great at asking for what she needed when going to sleep. As a seven-year-old, if she was lying in bed and she felt agitated, she would often jump up and say, 'I need to do handstands!' Trusting her inner knowledge around relaxation, I would invite her to do handstands for ten minutes which would often be accompanied by laughter and connection. Then, she would be ready to slow down and let her body move into relaxation.

We can also invite particular kinds of attachment play to support a child's natural relaxation process. Here are some ideas, gathered from parents and other Aware Parenting instructors:

## The Funny Reading Game

Reading books before bed is often a way that is used to suppress feelings. If this is the case, we can bring laughter and play into reading instead, so that it becomes a place for expression rather than suppression. If you are reading with your child, you can change the words to make it funnier. For example, 'the dog went to the toilet' instead of 'the dog went for a walk'. Each time they tell you what the book really says, you might say that you need special glasses to read the book. You could put mock glasses on and pretend that it makes you read words differently and make the words funny. Or you announce the end when you have just started or read it backwards.

## The Biting Books Game

When reading, you can pretend that the book bit you, and it jumps up in the air each time.

## It's Morning Game

You can pretend that instead of being evening, it is morning, and act surprised that they are in bed. Be goofy about all the morning things you are doing; tell them that breakfast is ready and what you have planned for the day, and so on! Act surprised when they insist that it is night-time and they are going to sleep!

## 'I-Hope-You-Aren't-in-Bed' Game

Announce loudly, 'I hope you aren't in bed!' and act surprised that they are. In a mock-angry voice, ask, 'What are you doing in bed!?' This can help with healing if you have got frustrated or angry in the past about them not going to bed!

## Tired-Eyes Game

You can say, 'Let's make sure our eyes don't close!' If they close their eyes, you can say in a mock surprised voice, 'You've got your eyes closed!' And you can also make big eyes and funny eyes and crossed eyes, and pull their arms gently to pretend to wake them up.

What happens if they are laughing and laughing, and then they suddenly start crying? Well, that is the second part of the natural relaxation process! The connection and the laughter created from the play also allow any other feelings to bubble out too.

*Connection, closeness and laughter help deeper feelings bubble up!*

### 3. Crying, Raging and Tantrums with Loving Support

Remember how Aware Parenting sees children's behaviour differently – and how whining, agitation, and crying over apparently small things – are not signs of tiredness but are part of the relaxation process. When a child (or adult) is tired, they are less able to repress feelings. Those feelings are trying to come out so that they can feel relaxed!

The old adage, 'it will all end in tears,' is so relevant here. Tears and tantrums are one of the most misunderstood relaxation processes. When our child is tearful, perhaps in response to something small or when we offer a Loving Limit, this is their wise body helping release the feelings that are sitting there, ready to be expressed. If we can be present and listen lovingly, they can express the feelings along with all the associated stress hormones and physical tension, and they can come out the other side after expressing those emotions, feeling much more relaxed.

Have you ever had a big cry with a loving friend or partner and felt deeply relieved and relaxed afterwards? Agitation is one of the main reasons that children find it hard to go to sleep and stay asleep, and they have these amazing natural release and relaxation (and healing processes) that we can cooperate with.

So, after play, your child might suddenly start crying. This is where you can stay with them, stay close, and listen lovingly. Offering your loving warmth and words, like, 'I'm here, I'm listening. You're letting it all out. I hear you. I'm right here with you.' As they let those feelings of the day, or week, or whenever from the past, out, they naturally return to a relaxed state. The crying might be loud and sweaty and big. There will probably be lots of vigorous movement of their arms and legs. That is their natural healing process in action (as long as we are there with them). This is the final part of recovery from the fight/flight/freeze process. This is the child releasing the feelings, tension and stress hormones that otherwise get in the way of them going to sleep and staying asleep until they've had enough sleep.

## Knowing When They Need to Talk, Play or Express Feelings

Because children have this inbuilt relaxation process, we can trust them to show us, and we can follow their lead. If they are jumping around and being silly, we can jump around and be silly with them! If they're telling us about their day, we can listen to them. If they are crying in response to something apparently small, we can listen to their tears. We can respond lovingly, *'I'm here with you. I'm listening. I see that you're upset.'* The younger the child, the more closeness they need when crying. Babies need to be held when crying for the crying to be healing.

- If our child wants to talk about their day, we can listen with our loving presence (bearing in mind that incessant talking can also be a way of suppressing deeper feelings).
- If they're having a rage or tantrum, we can stay close and listen lovingly.
- If they're hitting or biting, we can offer a Loving Limit and listen to their feelings.
- If they're playing and suddenly they start pinching, we can offer a Loving Limit and listen to their feelings.
- If they're laughing and suddenly the laughter turns to tears, we can move in close and listen lovingly.

## Loving Limits with Play

Sometimes our child will want to keep playing and playing, but they're clearly tired, or we're just not willing to play anymore. This is when we can offer a Limit (if it's because of our needs) or a Loving Limit (if their feelings are preventing them from sleeping): 'I see you really want to keep playing, sweetheart, and I'm only willing to play for 5 more minutes. Then I'm not willing to play anymore.' Often, the play and the Limit or the Loving Limit can help bring any deeper feelings to the surface. We can then lovingly listen to the feelings.

If they start getting rough in the play, again, we can offer a Loving Limit: 'I'm not willing for you to do that, sweetheart, and I'm right here, and I'm listening,' along with the minimum action to stop anyone getting hurt. And again, we can listen to the tears and feelings underlying the roughness.

## *Loving Limits with Attempts to Suppress Feelings*

Your child might want one thing, then another, then another, and they're still antsy. There might be requests for more games, more food, a change of scene. The ongoing agitation tells us that these are not needs but attempts to distract themselves from their feelings – they are communicating to us that they need help letting the feelings out. We can offer a Loving Limit, 'I see that you want another biscuit, sweetheart. I'm not willing to give you another biscuit, and I'm here, and I'm listening.' They might want you to read another ten books, and you can offer a Loving Limit after letting them know there's just one more. 'I really hear that you want me to read you another book, and I'm not willing to read any more books now, sweetheart. I'm here, and I'm listening.'

Returning to Pippa and Stacey, we could offer each of them a few suggestions. They could:

- Notice their child's tired signs.
- Offer loving connection as their child prepares for sleep, including more active physical connection through body contact games.
- Help their child release built up tension through attachment play and laughter or through crying and raging with physical movements. The crying and raging can be facilitated by either not suppressing their children's feelings in the ways they had done in the past, or offering Loving Limits when their child attempts to suppress their feelings.

In addition, breastfeeding can repress feelings and create mild forms of dissociation, which is generally a pleasant experience but can prevent deeper relaxation. Sucking itself creates dissociation, which is why breastfeeding, thumb sucking and dummies all can work as control patterns. In addition to this, breast milk contains wonderful hormones that help with that process. We want to clarify that we are passionate about breastfeeding and have found in working with many mothers over the years that listening to children's feelings can help breastfeeding be even more enjoyable for both mother and child, and can support even longer term breastfeeding because mothers don't give up in desperation, hoping that it will help with more sleep. In addition, because a baby or child is more present when they are feeding, it can be a more connecting experience, and mothers are less likely to feel resentful or drained when breastfeeding. Pippa and Stacey may want to breastfeed their sons before they get tired and then offer attachment play or listen to their feelings. Holding space for the tears before sleep will support that natural relaxation response. Using these practices can support both mothers to continue breastfeeding without having to stop completely in the hope of helping their child sleep more. We want to emphasise that if you enjoy breastfeeding your child to sleep, we support you to keep doing whatever you want to do. And, if you want to experiment with doing things differently and observe if this affects your child's sleep, relaxation and presence, we support you in doing that too. You can always go back to feeding to sleep again if you want to. This subject can be so controversial, and we want to remind you that we're offering you unconditional love and deep acceptance of whatever resonates with you and whatever you choose.

What about listening to feelings in the middle of the night? Parents are so welcome to do that. However, in our experience we have found the more children have the opportunity to release bigger feelings during the day and especially at night before bed, the less they wake at night to express feelings.

Please note – if you are happy breastfeeding through the night, we lovingly support your choice. We don't believe in telling parents what to do. We trust your innate sense of what is most helpful for your family.

## The Importance of Our Own State

Our own physical and emotional state in the evening has a huge effect on how much we can be attuned to our children, meet their needs for connection and cooperate with their natural relaxation processes so that they feel a true and natural sense of relaxation in their bodies, so that they can sleep restfully and sleep for as long as their body truly needs.

So our invitation is to be gentle with yourself. Is there something you're willing to do to help fill your cup in the early evening, such as five minutes of yoga or dancing around the kitchen?

## The Sleep Experiment

As with all of Aware Parenting, we invite you to approach this as an experiment. Would you like to change anything about your evenings? As you increase connection, play and listening to feelings, we invite you to observe your child. How is their sleep? What about tension or relaxation in their muscles? What about eye contact? How much do they move around at night? Are they smiling more? Notice if they are freer now to share their more painful feelings with you. Just like talking to a friend who can really hear us, once our children know we're going to listen to more of their painful feelings, they're likely to show us more of them. If you're tired or don't have the emotional spaciousness in you to offer attachment play or listen to feelings, you can always revert to your old sleep practices. Doing that might also be a helpful opportunity to clearly observe your child and see if you notice differences in them when you practice the two different ways.

## CHAPTER 9

# Suppression and Dissociation

*James walked into his 11-year-old son Sebastian's room and sighed. He knew the battle was about to begin, and he didn't know whether he had it in him for another one. Sebastian had headphones on, engrossed in the game he was playing on the computer. He started yelling to his friend, who was also online, 'You get it, go, you shoot it, do it, do it!'*

*This was Sebastian's nightly routine when he stayed at his dad's. When he returned from school, he went to his room and started gaming. He'd come out for dinner, not saying much and then he would go back until the bedtime battle started, which often finished with James yelling at Sebastian to get offline.*

*James was in two minds about what to do. One part of him wanted to give up. If Sebastian was gaming, he didn't bother James, so he could throw himself into working until late or sitting on the couch drinking Scotch until he fell asleep. It was easy to just ignore it – the pain of separating from Sebastian's other dad Rob was still very raw, and numbing it out was the easiest option right now. On the other hand, since the separation, he didn't feel connected with his son anymore. Sebastian lived most of the time with Rob and was focusing his anger about the separation towards James. It was clear that Sebastian preferred gaming to him, and he didn't want that to continue down the same non-existent relationship path he and his father had, full of pain and disconnection.*

*James reaches out and places a hand on Sebastian's shoulder. 'Hey mate, I want you to finish up now; it's late.' He felt his son bristle, and his heart ached. It didn't seem that long ago that his son wanted to spend every waking minute with him, the three of them were a happy family and now Sebastian was recoiling from him.*

*Sebastian grunts, 'I'm in the middle of this game. I can't finish now; I will lose all we have done – I need another half an hour!'*

*James feels torn. He has a deep desire for Sebastian to be happy, especially after how much hurt he has experienced recently. He also knows that half an hour may turn into an hour, and 11 p.m. bedtime for an 11-year-old is not ideal. Although he understands his son's passion for gaming, he can see that every time he plays, he disconnects from all that is happening around him.*

*James can see three options. 1) He can walk away, let his son keep playing, pour himself a drink and check out. 2) He can go for connection to help bridge the transition in getting off the computer. Or 3) he can offer a Loving Limit and hold space for the feelings that are likely to come when there is a loving 'no' for Sebastian to push up against.*

*James decides that he wants to offer some connection and healing to his son. He wants him to have autonomy and choice, yet he's also aware that Sebastian is suppressing his feelings through gaming. He knows how frustrated he would feel if he was engrossed in a work project, and someone just walked in and closed his laptop without him having a chance to complete what he was doing.*

*'I can see you want to finish this game, Seb. I really get that it is important to you. I'm willing for you to finish this level, and I'd love it if you'd teach me what you're doing. I have no idea how this all works. Would you show me?'*

*Sebastian stops what he is doing and looks at his dad. He was expecting a battle, but he can sense his dad's willingness to connect. He feels a bit wary, and his guard is still up, but he is open to seeing what*

> happens. 'Okay, Dad, I'll show you, but don't ask me too many questions. I need to concentrate.'
>
> James feels a sense of relief. This is a small step towards healing. He pulls up a chair and watches and occasionally comments.
>
> In time, Sebastian starts chatting away about the different levels and the skills he has. He tells his friend online that he is going to teach his dad how to play, and for the first time in a while, connection is happening between them. James can sense that Sebastian feels some power in being able to do something that he, James, isn't able to, and how important that is when he felt so powerless during the separation.

## Suppression in Action

Earlier in the book, we talked about the three options with feelings – expression, suppression (and dissociation), and aggression (and agitation). In the chapter on expression, we talked about how supporting children to express their feelings means that the feelings come out, literally leaving their bodies, helping them feel more relaxed and able to move on to the next thing (see Chapter 3). In the chapters on cooperation, aggression, fear and sleep (see Chapters 4–8), we showed what happens when feelings don't get to be expressed – how they accumulate, making cooperation and sleep hard, and how they sometimes show up as aggression and fear. In this chapter, we'll be exploring suppression and dissociation. Repetitive actions which cause suppression or dissociation are called 'control patterns' in Aware Parenting.

Before you read any more, we invite you to be compassionate with yourself as you read this chapter and to refrain from judging yourself or your children in relation to suppression and dissociation.

Marion shares her journey:

> When I first started practising Aware Parenting, I wanted to support my daughter in expressing a hundred per cent of her feelings. I wanted to make sure that she didn't ever suppress any feelings, ever! And I would judge myself when she did. That judgement of control patterns and judgement of myself actually got in the way of me giving her the kind of loving presence she needed to express her feelings.
>
> As the years went by, I found a very different way of thinking about suppression, dissociation and control patterns. I stopped judging them and chose to appreciate them instead. I was no longer willing to judge myself if my children were suppressing their feelings, which freed me up to be a whole lot more lovingly present with myself and them when they did! I'm grateful for suppression and dissociation, knowing how often they protect children (and adults) from being judged, shamed or outcast. I appreciate all the ways we find to not feel painful feelings, living in a world that doesn't welcome feelings and where most people aren't able to be lovingly present with feelings. I'm still passionate about helping myself and my children to express our feelings. But I no longer expect my children to be totally free from suppression or dissociation. I know that they do so a lot less than I do and that they are holding far fewer feelings inside than I am (after thirty-three-plus years of inner work!).

Finding deep compassion for suppression and dissociation can change everything. Our inner children feel the difference, as do our 'outer' children, who will experience a different quality from us when we're judging their control patterns and trying to get rid of them compared to when we want to deeply connect with them and to create the kind of environment which welcomes feelings naturally so that they have less need to suppress their feelings in the first place. This is different from giving up on the control pattern ever going away. This is a willingness to help our children feel more, express more and heal more without judgement, desperation or coercion.

## Uncomfortable Feelings Are Normal

From an Aware Parenting perspective, it is natural and normal for all children to experience painful feelings at times – no matter how much we aim to respond to their needs. Birth itself – even if a beautiful, calm experience – is a big event, and all babies have feelings during birth, and even more of them if the birth is traumatic. Babies regularly experience confusion and overwhelm. Children inevitably experience powerlessness and frustration when they're on a developmental cusp. Then there are daily stresses such as when parents and siblings are stressed or agitated, as well as regular events like going out in the car, visiting busy places or being with other children who might take things from them or hit them. Then there are experiences such as having a new sibling or moving house. For teens, the stresses of a changing body, friendships and romantic relationships and increasing awareness of what's happening in the world and their place in it can bring big emotions. Feelings are a normal, natural part of being a human being. As we've also shared, feelings are an integral part of the fight/flight response that happens when we perceive a threat, and expressing them completes the process so that our bodies don't need to stay in that stressed state.

Just as it's normal for all children to have feelings and to express them to heal, they also have an inbuilt ability to suppress them or dissociate from them when it might not be safe to express them. Without suppression, we wouldn't have survived as human beings. Just as crying, raging, and vigorous movements would have helped us heal from a near miss with a wild animal, being able to suppress or dissociate, be quiet, and be still, would have kept that child alive and safe if the wild animal was still prowling around the camp. Suppression and dissociation are vital and valuable.

Isn't our body incredible? It has all these ways to stop us from feeling feelings and keep us safe when those feelings are not welcomed. However, if we continue to suppress our feelings, it can affect our physical health.

Dr Gabor Maté, a world-renowned physician and expert on the effects of trauma, says:

> 'How does emotional repression predispose to illness? Since there is only one system, not four separate ones, whatever happens in any one part of it will affect the other parts. The repression of anger leads to the chronic secretion of stress hormones, such as cortisol, that suppress the immune system. The body's defences are disarmed against infection from the outside or malignant changes from within. When anger turns against the self, as it does in people unable to express it in a healthy way, hormonal imbalances can induce the immune system to mutiny against the body. Inflammatory autoimmune diseases of the joints, blood vessels and internal organs may follow, and even conditions like diabetes and Alzheimer's. It would be rare to find an individual with any of these diagnoses whose lifelong emotional coping patterns are not stamped by difficulty with anger.'[10]

We highly recommend his documentary 'The Wisdom of Trauma', which describes how connection, attunement and the expression of feelings are powerful elements in healing trauma and addiction.

## How Forms of Suppression are Acquired

There are two ways that babies and children learn to suppress feelings:

1. They learn directly from how we suppress their feelings; or
2. They find their own ways to suppress feelings.

### 1. Learned Suppression

Our relationship with our feelings will deeply affect our capacity to be present with our child's feelings in any moment. And our responses to their feelings will affect how they then respond to their own feelings. We want to remind you to put down the guilt sticks and be compassionate with yourself here. This isn't about trying to achieve some kind of non-existent perfection. This is about increasing compassionate understanding of our feelings, both as adults and children, as part of the journey of becoming more present with both.

Here are some examples of control patterns that adults use to dissociate from or suppress uncomfortable feelings:

- Eating when not hungry
- Drinking alcohol
- Being busy
- Over thinking
- Scrolling social media
- Shopping

Our relationship with our feelings and our own control patterns deeply affect how we respond to our baby, child or teen's feelings. If our child has uncomfortable feelings to express, but we repeatedly think they have an unmet need, we will, of course, do all we can to meet that need. We might think they are hungry and give them food. We might think they need movement and move or bounce them. We might think they need to suck and give them a dummy or pacifier.

Although it seems like the most compassionate thing to distract our babies and children from their painful feelings or interpret all of their feelings as indicating unmet needs, what we are really doing is distracting their awareness away from those feelings. The feelings don't go away – our child stops feeling the feelings because we have taken their attention away from their feelings and body. Those feelings stay in their body and accumulate over time. Those feelings have physiological correlates of stress hormones and physical tension which also relate to the fight/flight response, as we've discussed earlier in the book.

However, our distracting them has a further effect. Whatever we consistently do to distract our child from their feelings, they will internalise over time, so that when they feel those same uncomfortable feelings, they will ask for those same distractions. This can sometimes lead to a child seeming to need to be constantly 'entertained' (if we always entertain them when they need to cry), appearing to be hungry all the time (if we generally fed them when they had feelings to express), or needing to move around so much that they can hardly sit still (if we jiggled, rocked or bounced them when they were upset). Again, we invite you to put down any guilt sticks here!

Let's go into this in more detail. Eating to suppress feelings is commonly passed down in families. If your parents tended to eat when they were upset to prevent themselves from feeling uncomfortable feelings, then it's likely that:

1. They interpreted your painful feelings as hunger; and
2. They responded to your painful feelings by offering food, which led to
3. You interpreting your painful feelings as hunger; and then
4. You found it hard to differentiate between hunger and upset feelings, and then found yourself
5. Asking for food when you were upset, which led to you then
6. Eating when you were upset.

If you find it hard to differentiate between hunger and upset feelings, that suggests that might have been your experience. We think it is really important to bear this in mind – our child/ren learn these interpretations and responses from us. Here are some of the key ways that we distract babies and children from their feelings:

- Distraction – such as singing songs and reading books.
- Movement – jiggling, rocking, bouncing, driving them in the car.
- Giving them food when they're not hungry.
- Giving them a dummy or pacifier.

## 2. Finding Their Own Ways to Suppress Feelings

Babies and children suppress their feelings when we either don't understand that expressing feelings is healthy and necessary, or we don't realise that our child is trying to express painful feelings, or we aren't able to listen to those feelings because we are preoccupied, or full of our own upset feelings. Almost anything can become used to suppress feelings. Common control patterns in babies and children are:

- thumb or finger-sucking
- clutching a soft toy or a blanket
- pinching their skin
- getting in a particular position
- tensing up their muscles
- hair twirling
- using a screen to suppress
- incessant talking
- eating when not hungry
- ongoing nose-picking
- reading books to suppress feelings

Babies and children find these ways to suppress those feelings or dissociate from them when there isn't enough emotional presence and understanding of their feelings. They do that because feeling uncomfortable feelings without the loving support from an adult is unbearable for them. Feeling uncomfortable feelings is too much for a baby or child when they are physically alone, or when there isn't enough emotional presence, connection and listening or even the understanding that they are upset and have feelings to express. When children are young, it's easy to see control patterns in action. As children get older, suppression becomes more internal and socially acceptable, and isn't always as easy to see. Being able to see suppression is so powerful because we can literally see how our child is responding to their emotions.

## How Feelings Accumulate

Whatever percentage of their feelings we can be with, they can then express, and those feelings leave their bodies. Given the culture we live in and the time we grew up in, it is unlikely that any of us will be able to listen to a hundred per cent of our child's feelings, and whatever proportion we aren't able to listen to, they will need to suppress or dissociate from.

## How Suppression Changes Over Time

Over time, as babies become toddlers and children, these feelings accumulate more, and their control patterns can often evolve. For example:

- If we jiggle them, they might move whenever they're upset. *(Does that help you feel more compassion when your child won't sit at the dinner table?)*
- If we distract them through entertainment, they might need constant entertainment and never want to play alone. *(Does that help you feel more compassion when your child always wants you to play with them?)*
- If we feed them when they are upset they might ask for feeding and food when they're upset. *(Does that help you feel more compassion when your child asks for the fourth cup of juice?)*
- If we leave them to cry or don't have the availability or understanding to listen to their big feelings, they might carry a blanket or soft toy around everywhere. *(Does that help you feel more compassion when your seven-year-old still wants their teddy bear?)*
- If we give them a dummy or pacifier, they might want it more and more as their feelings accumulate. *(Does that help you feel more compassion when your four-year-old doesn't want to give it up?)*
- If we turn on a screen when they're upset, they might then use screens to repress feelings. *(Does that help you feel more compassion when your fifteen-year-old seems to be always looking at their phone?)*

Unless we listen to the underlying feelings, children will need to keep doing things to hold the feelings in or mildly dissociate from them. And as certain forms of suppression become less accepted as they get older, those suppression processes will morph. For example, thumb sucking might become nail-biting. As feelings accumulate, children need to do more and more to suppress those feelings. And as feelings accumulate, those suppressed feelings start to show up more and more in symptoms.

> *Susie was creating a magical craft structure. Her younger brother Johann came towards her, knocked it over and then took a piece and ripped it up. Susie felt outraged! He wrecked all her hard work! Her beautiful creation! She started raging at him, 'Don't EVER do that again!' Hearing the noise, their parents came in and yelled at Johann, 'We TOLD YOU not to do that, Johann!' Susie was really angry and getting louder. The parents moved into fix-it mode, 'Don't worry, Susie, just build another one!'*
>
> *Hearing this, Susie felt even MORE frustrated! She doesn't WANT to make another one! She rages louder. Susie's parents get frustrated as their own feelings arise, and her mum shouts out, 'Susie, it's just a piece of craft, why are you making such a big fuss about this! You can build another one!'*
>
> *Susie's feelings are not being heard or understood, and her crying gets louder. Susie's parents are also in their big feelings, 'Go to your room and don't come out until you calm down or can be happy again!' Susie retreats to her room, feeling hurt, powerless, and scared, but those feelings are too overpowering when she's on her own, so she needs to do something with them.*

In the above scenario, we can see how Susie's unexpressed anger may turn into aggression. She may start breaking things in her room, kicking the wall, or throwing things. Or she may get her blanket, clutch on to it, and rub it back and forth along her arm, feeling nothing but a kind of pleasant numbness.

The same dissociation can emerge when Susie is an adult. When she feels frustrated or experiences not being heard or understood, she might drink alcohol to numb herself. She might keep so busy with work that she doesn't have any space to feel. She may turn to smoking, drugs, online shopping, or anything that means not feeling the painful feelings, not realising that the source of this behaviour is from many years before.

How could we respond to Susie in that situation?

We might say, 'Oh Susie, your brother broke the creation you'd put so much time into making … I am so sorry that I didn't get here in time to stop that happening (thank you again to Patty Wipfler of Hand in Hand Parenting for this phrase) … I'm here with you … I'm listening.' And then we can wait, holding space for her to express her outrage, doing what we can to stay calm. As Susie feels, expresses and moves through those big feelings, we could offer her empathy, acknowledge her feelings, and give her a hug if she's willing to receive it. After the feelings have been felt and expressed we may offer, 'What can I do to help you? What do you need?' We could go to her brother, Johann, and find out what was going on for him to cause that behaviour, and when he's ready and willing, to find a way to repair with Susie.

## Helping Children Express Their Feelings

For children to be able to feel, express and release feelings of overwhelm, frustration, confusion, sadness, and all the other myriad of feelings, we need to:

1. Understand that expressing feelings is natural, healthy and healing.
2. Have the emotional spaciousness to stay compassionately present in our own body whilst they are expressing those feelings.
3. Respond in ways that help them express their feelings.

Again, we invite you to be compassionate with yourself here. Most of us grew up in families that didn't welcome crying and raging. Most of us grew up in families where the adults couldn't stay present in their bodies when we were feeling and expressing big feelings. Most of us didn't hear things like, 'I welcome all your feelings. I'm here and listening' when we were crying or raging. Being able to do all three of these requires a lot and often involves quite a long learning journey for us as adults.

For us to be present in our bodies when our child is crying, we need to stay present with similar feelings in ourselves. If our parents couldn't be present with our tears, or our frustration, we would have found ways to repress those feelings or dissociate from them.

### How Can We Tell if Suppression is Happening?

*If a child often does a certain thing when they are clearly upset (e.g. they've fallen over), or when they're tired (which is when upset feelings bubble to the surface to be expressed), and their eyes look a bit glazed, then it tells us that they may be amid suppression or dissociation. These behaviours are like flags – indications that uncomfortable feelings are bubbling up to the surface but aren't being expressed.*

We invite you to observe your child. What do they frantically want? Often when they desperately want something, that something helps them dissociate from their feelings; 'I NEED to have that chocolate,' or 'GIVE me the iPad!' Often, because of the frantic energy, you might find yourself giving it to them quickly because it usually keeps them quiet and stops the big feelings from coming out. But this can just push more feelings inside, which means that they need to do more to not feel them, or instead, those feelings come bursting out in agitation or aggression and can show up as hitting or biting other children or other forms of harshness.

If our child isn't letting their feelings out, you may see them space out when they get upset. They may become reliant on a blanket or a bottle or want food or sweets whenever they get upset. They may want the iPad and insist they must watch their show NOW! It can be computer games for older kids, or it can be busyness where they can't sit still.

*The more we observe suppression, the easier it becomes to see. You might notice when your child is biting their nails, when their eyes are glazed, or when they have that urgent quality to the tone of their voice that tells you feelings are sitting underneath. You might also clearly see suppression and dissociation much more clearly in the adults around you, too (including yourself!)*

We can support children to stay present with their feelings by:

1. Observing them and learning to perceive when our child feels upset and letting them know that we are there with them and are listening.
2. Coming in close whilst staying present in our body instead of distracting them.
3. We can increase our own ability to stay in our bodies with uncomfortable feelings which will help us to be more comfortable being present with them whilst they're feeling and expressing feelings. To do that, we generally need to have another adult be present with us when we are feeling upset. As we experience that loving presence when we feel sad or frustrated or overwhelmed or confused or outraged, we feel increasingly comfortable with staying connected with the sensations in our body. This person might be an empathy buddy – another adult who can hold space for our feelings. We explain more about empathy buddies in Chapter 10.
4. In turn, this means our child feels our compassionate presence, and we can support and facilitate the expression of their feelings through simply listening, or offering a Loving Limit if necessary.

This is no small step. This is the next step in a very long journey of humanity. We invite you to have profound compassion for yourself in your own unique feelings path.

## The Process of Helping Children Suppress Fewer Feelings

The wonderful thing is that whatever your age or your child/ren's age, it is never too late to increase your capacity to feel your feelings and help them increase that for themselves too. Remember that suppressed feelings stay in the body, affecting us in many ways. However, expressing feelings allows them to move through our bodies and leave us. When we can be fully present with our child's feelings, they can feel them and express them and those feelings leave them. The fewer pent-up feelings we have and the less we need to suppress them or dissociate from, the more connected, relaxed, peaceful, loving and clear we feel. And it is the same for our children. The fewer suppressed feelings they have, the more connected, relaxed, peaceful, loving and clear they feel, which profoundly affects their behaviour.

We'd love to say again: We can value our ways of suppressing feelings and dissociating from them whilst *also* increasing our spaciousness to be present with more and more of our feelings and our child's too.

Our level of comfort with seeing our child using control patterns will be unique for each of us. For each of us, there will be a level of suppression that we are comfortable with and a level at which we want to step in and do something. For example, you might be comfortable with your child suppressing their feelings for half an hour on the screen, but not for three hours. You might be willing for them to suppress their feelings with one cookie, but not a whole packet. You might be happy for them to suppress through reading for two hours but not four. We invite you to notice where you feel willing for your child to suppress their feelings and where you are not. You might find that suppression becomes a particular issue when it interrupts sleep, affects their health, or develops into other destructive behaviours in the teenage years.

Here are some things you might find helpful:

1. **When we observe our child suppressing feelings, we can choose these ways of thinking about it. We can:**

- Understand the cause of suppression and have compassion for ourselves and our children.
- Choose a compassionate way of thinking about ourselves and our parenting. This helps us be more available, loving and present to listen to their feelings!
- Stop judging it. Judgement is likely to lead to a strong impulse to get rid of it, which also doesn't give the kind of quality most conducive to children expressing feelings.
- Perceive suppression as a flag for feelings. Whenever your child picks their nose or twirls their hair or sucks their thumb, it is a flag, telling you that uncomfortable feelings are arising. This way of thinking about them can help us respond with loving presence.
- Understand that it may take time for our child to change their understanding and perception and to feel freer to feel and express their feelings again.

2. **We can support ourselves to feel calm and relaxed:**

- This includes expressing our own feelings about their control patterns to another adult. We may also have feelings from the past bubbling up, especially if we had a similar control pattern as a child, e.g. if our child sucks their thumb, it will be important that we get to express our own feelings and memories of sucking our thumb.
- Doing whatever we can to ensure our *needs cup* isn't empty, and our own *painful feelings backpack* isn't full. Babies and children are intimately in tune with our emotional state and are much less likely to share their feelings with us if we are depleted or in lots of emotional pain ourselves.

## 3. We can offer our loving presence:

- We can move in to connect with them with our loving presence. The antidote to suppression is connection. In practical terms, this can mean things like coming close, offering eye contact and gentle touch and the quality of presence in our attention on them. The beautiful thing is that children internalise how we respond to them. So the more we can offer an unconditionally loving presence to them when they're suppressing feelings, the more they will internalise that unconditional love for themselves.

- Loving presence also includes an appreciation for control patterns. Rather than trying to get rid of them, the aim is more to offer the conditions that will help our child be freer to express the underlying feelings and therefore less likely for them to use control patterns.

- We might say things like, 'I know you needed to put your fingers in your mouth when we took your sister to school in the car, and I couldn't listen to your feelings then. I'm sorry. I'm here now, and I'm listening.'

- Or 'I understand that you really want to watch the screen. I remember giving you screen time yesterday when you really wanted me to play with you. I'm here now and I'm listening.'

## 4. We can use attachment play:

Attachment play, which we explored in Chapter 3, is often really helpful in loosening up feelings that are held in suppression. Bringing in connection and play helps release lighter feelings and helps the child know that we love them and are there to help them when they are suppressing feelings. The wonderful thing about attachment play is that it offers a special kind of warm connection, often added to a dose of laughter. When we find these ways of connecting with our children, they will feel connected with us. Being connected to us also means connecting with themselves, their body, and their feelings. That's how attachment play works. It offers connection, and in most of the nine forms there's also laughter. Laughter helps create a special kind of warm connection. Laughter also releases feelings like light fears, powerlessness, frustration, feeling unsure, and so on.

So, when we get in and do attachment play with whatever our child is suppressing, we're helping them connect with themselves and their body and connect with us (which they need to be able to do to let out the feelings), and we're helping them release lighter feelings that are sitting on the surface.

For example:

**'NO (suppression) on the couch!':** For this one, the child is on the couch, and we say, 'Whatever you do, DON'T suck your thumb when I turn around, will you?' And they say, 'noooo'. We turn away, pretend to whistle and be all nonchalant, and turn around, and suddenly we see them sucking their thumb, and we say in a really mock silly voice, 'Nooooooo! You said you wouldn't suck your thumb!' And repeat!

Marion says:

> *I remember a session with a mother and her two children, both of whom picked their noses. We spent about forty-five minutes doing attachment play. I would say, 'What flavour bogie/booger is that? Strawberry?' And they'd eagerly say, 'YES!' And I'd say, 'You're not trying to trick me, are you?' And they'd smilingly say, 'NO!' And then I'd encourage them to get a bogie/ booger, and I'd pretend (PRETEND!) to eat it and say, 'NOOOOO, that wasn't strawberry, that was vomit flavour! EEERGH!!!' And they would laugh and laugh! And we'd do this over and over and over again.*
>
> *Each time I'd ask them, 'You're not going to trick me THIS time, are you?' We laughed for forty-five minutes. It was SO FUN! And if you think, 'I don't want to spend forty-five minutes on this!' I hear you AND I invite you to think of what an amazing thing this is. This helps free up all the feelings that will otherwise stay inside their bodies and lead to all the other things you find most annoying!*

Sometimes, repeated attachment play might be enough to dissolve the suppression. But sometimes, the suppression might hold many more and bigger feelings at bay. In which case, the attachment play often opens the doors for those bigger feelings to emerge.

Like a pressure cooker, letting off steam of the lighter feelings with laughter, coupled with the warm, loving connection of the play, space is made for bigger feelings to come out in tears and tantrums.

## 5. We can listen to the feelings and offer Loving Limits:

- **Listening to crying, raging and tantrums:** Often, the play facilitates the deeper, more painful feelings to emerge – the rage and the loss and the sadness and the grief and the frustration – those all come out in tears and raging tantrums. This is what happened with the children Marion was playing with in the story above. One of the children suddenly moved into a huge cry, with her mother listening, whilst Marion stayed with the other child. The mother saw a big difference in her child after the big cry.

- **Loving Limits with the suppression:** This is another possibility – that you offer a Loving Limit with the suppression. This is possible if the suppression is a dummy/pacifier, soft toy, or screen, but not if it is muscle tension or thumb sucking. However, if you do choose to do this, we recommend having a lot of caution, awareness and observation.

We recommend starting with attachment play with the suppression, ideally for several days or more. And if you are going to offer a Loving Limit, we recommend giving your child notice. For example, in the morning, you might explain that that night, you are going to help them to go to sleep without their control pattern. We wouldn't suggest going cold turkey.

For your child, that particular form of suppression has potentially been holding in a lot of feelings, and suddenly taking that away, even if you then listen to some of the feelings, is likely to mean that once you've listened to as much crying and raging as you can, that your child still has a whole load of feelings. So they will either need to keep crying or find a new way to suppress the feelings. This is why understanding and appreciating suppression is so important.

For instance, we might tell them that we're not willing for them to go on a screen right before bed. Then we can listen to the feelings. 'I hear that you really want the screen, sweetheart, and I'm not willing for you to go on it now, and I'm here, and I'm listening,' and then listening to the big feelings that show up. But also knowing that if the suppression has been around a long while, one cry isn't going to release all the feelings that the suppression has been holding in, so we might need to give it back to them, e.g. if it's a dummy. If we remove the suppression without supporting them in expressing their feelings, they might need to acquire a different form of suppression, possibly one deeper in the body that's harder to work with. We don't ever recommend pulling their finger out of their mouth if thumb or finger sucking is a control pattern.

## 6. We can look at the longer term:

It may be that once your child has expressed a lot of feelings, they don't tend to use that control pattern regularly except for really stressful times – so the control pattern becomes again a flag for feelings, an indication that our child is needing more from us to express those feelings in healthy ways so that they can return to more presence and balance.

## The Correlation Between Our Suppression and Our Child/ren's

When you see your child's ways of suppressing emotions, does this help you see yours more clearly and compassionately? Seeing how we suppress feelings can help us be compassionate with the younger parts of us who didn't grow up in a culture where feelings were welcomed and seen as normal, natural and beautiful.

Do you notice your child/ren's go-to forms of suppression, and have you ever noticed a correlation between theirs and yours? There isn't always a direct correlation, but sometimes there can be!

We'd also love to say that almost any of the things in the list below can be used to suppress feelings at times, but at other times can be used to meet needs. For example, screens can be used to meet needs for learning, stimulation, creativity, community, connection, and so much more. Just as eating food can be used to nourish and fuel our bodies at times, and at other times can be used to distract ourselves from our feelings.

- If your child has a dummy or pacifier, do you tend to stop yourself from expressing your feelings to others? Or do you tend to tense up around your mouth or bite your nails when you've got feelings bubbling?
- If your child repeatedly asks for food when they're upset, do you tend to eat to suppress your feelings?
- If your child moves around a lot when they're upset, do you tend to get busy or do exercise to suppress feelings?
- If your child asks to be entertained when they're upset, do you tend to entertain yourself with YouTube or a book or social media to distract yourself from your feelings?
- If your child sucks their thumb or fingers when they're upset, do you tend to bite your nails or put your hands to your mouth before you've even noticed feelings coming up?
- If your child wants to be alone when they're upset, do you tend to want to be on your own when you feel stressed or depressed?

And this doesn't only apply to suppression. We can also often learn things about ourselves and others when we see our responses to our children.

- If we see a parent punishing their raging child in the supermarket, we might wonder whether they punish themselves internally with self-judgement, self-shaming or guilt.
- If we see a parent threatening to leave their child when the child is crying, we might wonder if they leave themselves emotionally when they have painful feelings.
- If we see a parent doing everything they can to distract a child from painful feelings, we might wonder whether they also distract themselves when they have painful feelings.

This can be really helpful in increasing our compassion for other parents. If you are seeing another parent do something you wouldn't do, you might be curious whether what they are doing might reflect what they are doing to themselves internally and what was done to them when they were little.

When we imagine the little people inside each of us, it can help us more easily find compassion, as well as clarity! If you have painful feelings coming up now, we want to remind you:

*It is never too late to listen to the feelings of babies, children or adults!!!*

## Working with Suppression as an Adult

As we talked about earlier in this chapter, we have found unconditionally loving ourselves when we're suppressing or dissociating has been transformational for ourselves and our clients. If we had kept on crying or raging as children, we might have been punished, shamed or judged in some way. The suppression of feelings is then a form of self-protection and self-preservation which comes from needs to be safe, to belong and be loved. Sometimes, it might have been that the adults around us simply didn't understand how we felt or didn't understand that feelings are healthy and natural. Or it might have been that their big feelings were close to the surface, and they might have raged or reacted in big or harsh ways if we kept on crying or raging.

Often those protective parts of us have been judged, and rarely have they been appreciated. Appreciating them often leads to big shifts. If we're judging them and trying to push them away and get rid of them, they're likely to believe that they need to do more to keep us safe and will ramp up their efforts.

For most of us, the family and culture we grew up in didn't understand that feelings are helpful or didn't have the capacity to be with their own feelings or be with our feelings. They may have grown up in a culture that saw feelings as misbehaviour or that feelings always communicated an unmet need. To the extent to which there weren't adults around us who could be present with our feelings and listen to them lovingly, we needed to either suppress them or dissociate from them, depending on the bigness of those feelings.

So we can see these processes as parts of ourselves protecting us. If we didn't stop crying, we might have been shamed or punished or judged or excluded. The more these parts of us feel our love for them, the more trust they will have that we have compassion now to be with the feelings they were set up to prevent us feeling and expressing. We might choose to communicate with our control pattern in the following ways:

- 'I appreciate all the times you helped me when there was no one there who could listen.'
- 'Thank you for keeping me safe.'
- 'I'm sorry for the times I judged or tried to just get rid of you. I didn't realise how much you wanted to help me.'

We might say:

- 'Thank you so much for wanting to protect me. I'm going to see if I have the spaciousness and presence now to listen to the feelings, but would you stay close in case I need you?'
- 'I so appreciate that you cared for me by suppressing the feelings.'

Would you like to play with these phrases by imagining a moment when you might move to a control pattern and then put your hand on your heart and speak the words? We can ask ourselves if we can be with the feeling, and if we aren't able to or don't want to, we can choose to go on and suppress the feelings. Wouldn't you have loved to have heard the following when you were suppressing feelings:

- 'I love you, whether you are feeling and expressing a feeling or suppressing a feeling.'

- 'I trust that you know how much presence you have to be with a feeling and how much connection you're feeling from the adults around you.'
- 'You don't need to hold those feelings in anymore, sweetheart. I'm here with you and your feelings are not too much for me.'

Loving presence is the antidote for suppression, whether we're a child or an adult!

## Digital Technology as a Form of Suppression

We particularly want to mention the use of technology in this chapter. In the opening story about 11-year-old Sebastian and his dad, James, we talked about how screens can be a powerful way to suppress feelings. From a young age, children can use screens to suppress feelings, which we might see when a two-year-old wakes up, and the first thing they say is, 'I want the iPad!'

Many adults have screens as control patterns – online shopping, scrolling social media, watching one YouTube video after another or even online pornography. When we understand how suppression works, we can also understand why many children get so angry or upset when we ask them to turn off the computer or the iPad. The bubbling feelings suppressed by the screen use now come pouring out.

We don't believe that screens are enemies. We both deeply value screens. They provide us with ways to connect with people all over the world in our work, and we both run workshops, courses and sessions through the medium of digital technology. We have both experienced connection, fun and attachment play with our children and teens and screens.

Offering one-to-one time playing online games can be a gorgeous way to bring in power-reversal games, with the teens or tweens having much more understanding and skill than we do. This reverses the usual balance of power where we usually know more and can do more. This play can bring lots of healing laughter. As we saw in Sebastian and James' story, Sebastian teaching his dad how to play the game was an easy way for him to have more knowledge, skill and power.

Asking your tweens or teens to teach you how their favourite game or app works can be a powerful way for them to teach you something. There can also be fantastic opportunities for family connection and laughs by watching funny animal videos, creating dances or doing something together on TikTok. Digital technology can be a wonderful way to create connection.

We want to remind you how this is the case with many forms of suppression. Food is essential for survival, but we can also eat when we're not hungry to suppress feelings. Movement is necessary for health, but we can also move constantly to distract ourselves from what's happening in our bodies. Screens are not essential for humans, but they can meet many needs such as learning, community, and entertainment – whilst also being profoundly powerful in their capacity to distract our attention away from our bodily sensations, including our feelings.

We can use screens to dissociate and numb our feelings at any age. This is more likely to be the case if we use them on our own. There are two ways that digital technology is such a powerful medium for suppression to happen. The first is because it is so engaging and ongoing, so it can help us suppress/dissociate far more deeply and for much longer than if we ate some chocolate, for example. The second is because of the reward/dopamine cycle, especially in gaming and pornography.

Many studies have concluded the strong link between a person experiencing hyperarousal while playing video games or watching pornography, and the brain associating the activity with dopamine. Dopamine is a powerful neurotransmitter in the brain. Dopamine communicates with brain cells and encourages them to act in a pleasurable, excitable, euphoric way. A person develops a strong drive to seek out that same pleasure again and again which is why gaming and pornography can become addictive.

In our experience, technology and screens aren't necessarily the cause of challenges. Rather, it is more often the lack of connection in a relationship that fuels a profound suppression, dissociation or even addiction. When children have the opportunity to express their feelings, spend quality time with the ones they love and feel valued and seen for who they are, they are much more likely to moderate their own technology use.

You may also be thinking about your relationship with screens and how you reach for your phone when you have feelings bubbling. As with all the forms of suppression we have mentioned, meeting this with awareness and compassion is the first step in shifting your relationship with your feelings.

## Being Freer from Suppression

Although listening to our baby, child or teen's feelings can be really hard, supporting them in suppressing fewer feelings can have wonderful effects. The less suppression or dissociation they need to do, the more they can live in the present moment and feel the sensations in their bodies and their feelings. They're more capable of deep connection. They have more presence and awareness, and make more eye contact. They have more awareness of their body and movements, so they know their capacities and are less likely to have accidents or fall over. They also develop greater resilience and courage to step out of their comfort zone as they have evidence that they are safe to do things that are hard and that any feelings they feel will be welcomed.

They have more capacity to concentrate for long periods on one thing. They have more compassion for their own feelings and the feelings of others, both because they internalise that from us and because less accumulated feelings means more natural warmth. They're more likely to be able to stay with their bodily sensations when they have uncomfortable feelings. They're more likely to be able to sit still and sleep without fidgeting and sleep until they have had enough sleep. They're more likely to be naturally gentle and cooperate more.

Wow! What a big chapter this has been! We wonder how you're feeling now. The next section is about us, the parents, and you might have the sense of needing that after reading this. See you there!

# Part III
# Reparenting Ourselves

'Parenting our children with compassionate understanding can inspire us to reparent our inner children in the same way.'

~ Marion

CHAPTER 9

# Repair and Compassion

Lael remembers:

*Merel sat opposite me, expressing a mixture of sadness and rage. Sad because her relationship with her fourteen-year-old son Bailey was strained and angry because he was treating her harshly.*

*'Doesn't he know that all I do is for him? Being a single mother isn't easy – the last year has been so hard. Since his father left, I have been juggling the bills, the house and my own hurt and grief, and all I get from him is how he doesn't have enough cool stuff or complaints when I ask him to do the smallest thing. He has no idea how much I am trying to hold it together. And all I cop from him is a bad attitude. He is so ungrateful.'*

*Merel is trying to fight back the tears. Her body is tense, she is angry, but I can see she doesn't want to express the anger, nor move to the sadness. She clenches her fists as she speaks and wants to keep coming back to why Bailey should change and what suggestions I have to make him do as she asks.*

*'The other week, I asked him to unpack the dishwasher, I had made dinner, and it was a simple request. Well, it was like I had asked him to clean the entire house from top to bottom without taking a break! He completely lost it, swearing and yelling at me, telling me I should do it. He told me I was a terrible mother and many other hurtful things. And I snapped. I screamed back, and we both ended up yelling. I asked him to apologise, and he refused. He finally walked off and slammed his door,*

*and we really haven't spoken to each other since. That was nine days ago, and we are now at this point where it's almost better to not look at each other and only communicate via text message. I am so angry, I can't get past it. I know I am the adult, but this fills me with rage.'*

*I empathised with Merel about how frustrated she feels and acknowledged how much she is holding. I expressed my compassion for her with the challenges she is facing. The more I gave her empathy, the more she softened, and the tears started to fall, as she expressed the pain that she was feeling.*

*I asked her to tell me more about her feelings. Were they were familiar to her from somewhere?*

*'I know this feeling well; it's how I used to feel when I was with my dad all the time. He was a very closed man. My mother died when I was young, and there wasn't much space for expressing feelings. I had to do so many things in my family, I would take care of my younger brothers and cook meals, and he never really thanked me. Whenever I asked for something, he would say no or fly off the handle. He would always say, "You don't know how lucky you kids are with a roof over your head and food to eat." I was grateful, but I wanted more. Some affection or some thanks. I don't think I was asking for much. I left home as soon as possible, even though it meant leaving my brothers behind, but I couldn't handle his anger and harshness. I know it was hard for him. My mum was the one that did all the nurturing, and I think when she died, it kind of broke him, so he just closed up and stayed angry.'*

*I asked Merel if she could link her feelings as a child with how she feels towards her son now. When her son didn't show gratitude or didn't want to do what she asked, was it reminding her of those feelings she had when she was younger?*

'I get why you are saying that, and I can see the link – but I just can't stop flying off the handle. It makes me so mad. Can't Bailey see how lucky he has it? A mum that is kind and shows interest in his life and hardly asks him to do much at all. If only he could have seen how hard it was for me.'

Merel and I discuss how her rage and anger are feelings she could never express. When her dad dismissed her or shut her down, her rage and anger got held inside. She needed to push it down because there was no-one there to listen, and now as a parent in similar situations, all the rage and anger she never got to express is coming out.

I asked Merel what she wished could have happened when she was younger.

'Well, for one thing, I just needed someone to hug me and listen to how sad I was. I never got to grieve for my mum. All the adults around me just freaked out and tried to keep me busy or tell me that it was my job now to look after my brothers. I was only thirteen and needed someone to listen to me. I also just needed to be a kid and not have this responsibility. What I really wanted was a place to express how unfair it all was. I needed someone who wouldn't judge me or tell me to get over it. I just longed for a soft place to land with all my feelings.'

As Merel shared this part of her life, I asked her if she could connect in with her son. She took some breaths and more tears began to fall as she shared what she realised.

'Oh gosh, my son is me. He is feeling lost and hurt. We haven't really discussed his dad leaving. I can't believe that I am doing similar things that my dad did. My pain is stopping me from turning up for him. He's not doing this deliberately. He is just hurting.

*Why couldn't I see this? Why couldn't I give him what he needed? I know how painful that is.'*

*Merel let herself really get the bigness of what she was understanding. The generational hurts that are often passed on, the pain that we don't get to express, then turns up in the next generation. Her body softened as she talked about Bailey and all he might be feeling. She linked the threads of his pain and hurt to her pain and hurt. She saw that her role as his parent is to not take it out on him but do her own healing so she can respond to him from her adult self so that he could then heal.*

I offered to Merel that she and Bailey were just trying to bring about healing. He was looking for a safe adult to express his big feelings (thanks to being asked to unpack the dishwasher), and she was looking for a place to feel and express the hurt from her upbringing.

As Merel began to understand why she was responding the way she was, feelings of guilt and shame started to arise. 'Oh gosh, I can't believe how I have been treating Bailey. I'm the parent here, and I've been acting like a hurt child. What kind of mother does that?'

I assure her that at some point in time, we all do that as a parent. Nobody comes to parenting with a clean slate, we all have hurts and pain, and often our children bring those feelings to the surface. Our invitation is to understand our stories, do the healing work and step into compassion and understanding for ourselves. I remind Merel that she is doing the best job she knows how with the life story she has. More judgements, shame and guilt will only create disconnection. If she can meet these parts of herself (and the younger parts of herself) with compassion and empathy, she is more likely to bring empathy to her son too.

We discuss ways to repair with Bailey. Merel begins to see the power she has to repair and how that helps him learn about taking responsibility *when we've acted in harsh ways to others. She sees that it is her role as the parent to facilitate this repair. It is never Bailey's role to take responsibility for her needs and feelings. It is her responsibility to own her feelings and be with the parts that have showed up.*

*Merel shared with me a week later that after our session, she went home and gently and compassionately approached Bailey. She said that he was wary at first, expecting an angry mother, but when she spoke with gentleness and with her heart open, he softened pretty quickly. She apologised for her reactions and said that she wanted to make it safe enough for Bailey to bring those big feelings that he may be having to her. She wanted to work as a team and create space for him to express how he was feeling about his dad and other aspects of his life. She said that they spoke for nearly an hour (the longest conversation they'd had in nearly two years), and they both cried and agreed to owning their feelings more. Merel shared that the explosive interaction was the best thing to happen as it actually brought them back to each other.*

## Repairing in the Moment

The inner work we will be inviting you to do is all about healing from past hurts, because the more we do that, the more availability we have to offer reparative experiences to our children in the present. As we have touched on throughout this book – there is no such thing as a perfect parent. As Marion likes to say, the idea of perfect parenting is created by the Disconnected Domination Culture, and is designed to train us to pick up those guilt and shame sticks. As you may have discovered by reflecting on your own childhood and how your parents raised you – they were doing the most they could do at that moment, given the culture, family and time they grew up in. As are you.

The journey of parenting asks us to heal our past, so we can be who we want to be in the present. When we think we need to be 'perfect', the belief in which is a part of Disconnected Domination Culture conditioning, we set ourselves up for immense pressure and internal criticism when it doesn't all go to plan. When we embrace ourselves wholeheartedly when we act from our younger parts and past hurts, we give ourselves self-compassion and the opportunity to develop true resilience and inner strength.

We also model to our children what they can do when they behave in a way that is hurtful for another. Doing so, we teach our children about repair, self-compassion and possibility. It is so important for children to learn how to repair and when we show an authentic expression of this, it is more likely that children will move towards repair naturally and of their own volition.

## The Repair Process

How can we repair after we've behaved in painful ways?

There are four steps to the repair process:

1. Compassion for ourselves and why we did what we did.
2. Empathy for our child and how they felt when we did what we did.
3. Taking responsibility and apologising without guilt.
4. Offering a reparative experience.

### 1. Compassion for ourselves and why we did what we did

If we are judging, shaming, guilting or punishing ourselves after doing something painful to our child, it's going to be really hard to repair with our child.

Marion calls self-judgement 'emotional sticks'. When we hit ourselves with those sticks, we feel emotional bruises. We learnt these ways of responding to our own painful behaviour when we were children. The adults around us didn't understand that our behaviour was caused by our thoughts, needs and feelings and we were conditioned to believe that we needed to be judged, shamed, punished or guilted so we wouldn't do that again. We internalised those responses and then do them to ourselves.

When we feel those emotional bruises of shame and guilt, our attention is taken up by them, perhaps to a point where they are all-consuming. Whilst we're doing that to ourselves, we have little available empathy to offer our child. If we say, 'I'm a terrible mother for doing that,' our children will sense our shame. You might even notice yourself saying things like, 'I shouldn't have done that. I'm so bad.' However, when we do that, our children may learn to judge and shame themselves when they act in hurtful ways.

Gradually learning to respond with self-compassion, perhaps even pinpointing the thoughts, needs or feelings that led to our behaviour, means we will have much more compassion available for ourselves and for our child. More empathy means more likelihood of healing happening.

*Invitation for Reflection: We invite you to remember a time recently when you acted in a way that you wish you hadn't with your child. What was underneath that behaviour? What were you thinking/believing at that time? Did you have any unmet needs? Were some feelings bubbling up from the past for you?*

As you connect with the answers to these questions, do you feel some compassion for yourself? What tangible thing could you do next time to help you stay connected with self-compassion? How could you think more helpful thoughts, meet your needs more in the moment, and get to express those feelings in healthy ways?

## 2. Empathy for our child and how they felt when we did what we did

The next step is to listen to our child's feelings. Again, if we are hitting ourselves with those shame sticks and are repeating, 'I'm sorry, I'm sorry,' from that place of shame, we aren't likely to have much availability to listen to how it was for our child. Empathy requires spaciousness so that they can express how they feel. This expression might take many forms, depending on your child's age and many other factors. They may move directly into suppression, aggression or expression:

- **Expression:** They might start crying or raging, in which case we can simply listen lovingly, offering our loving presence and nodding, 'I hear you. I understand how upset you are. I'm listening.' They might be expressing how they feel in words, such as, 'I hate you / I don't like it when you do that / that's not fair.' Again, we can listen lovingly and reflect back what we hear; 'I hear that you hate me / I understand that you don't like it when I do that / That really wasn't fair, was it?' It's really important to keep holding compassion for ourselves. Otherwise, we're likely to flip into justifying why we did it, reacting, or moving into judgement or power-over. Then we keep listening to their feelings for as long as we can listen, and ideally until they move out the other side of the feelings.

- **Aggression:** They might start hitting or throwing things. Remember, with aggression, we have two choices – attachment play or Loving Limits. If you go with attachment play, power-reversal games are really helpful for repair – especially if we've used power-over them (see Chapter 6). If laughter happens, they are releasing the fear they felt when you did whatever it was that you did. If the aggression continues, you will probably want to offer a Loving Limit to say no to the behaviour and yes to the underlying feelings. You might take the minimum action to stop the hitting, such as holding their hand and saying, 'I'm not willing for you to hit me, and I'm here, and I'm listening.'

- **Suppression or dissociation:** If they go really quiet, avoid eye contact, start sucking their thumb, or want to go on their iPad, then we invite you to move in close. Remember, the antidote to suppression is connection! You might offer empathy, 'Are you feeling upset/shocked/scared? I'm here. I'm listening.' You might also offer some power-reversal games. For example, if you spoke loudly or harshly, you might invite them to shout at you whilst you jump in the air each time they do.

*Invitation for Reflection: Going back to what you were remembering, how did your child respond afterwards? What could you do or say to show them that you were listening to their feelings?*

## 3. Taking responsibility and apologising without self-judgement

Children will often take responsibility for our reactions, so it is really important to give them clear information that they are not responsible for our actions, feelings or needs. Instead, we can take responsibility for these without shaming ourselves. So, we let them know that it wasn't their fault. It's also important that we apologise without judging ourselves, to let them know that we're sorry that we did what we did, e.g. 'I'm so sorry that I spoke to you like that, sweetheart. I had some really big feelings. It wasn't your fault. You didn't do anything wrong. It's my job to care for my feelings, and I didn't do that. I care about treating you with respect, and I didn't do that.'

*Invitation for Reflection: What would you have liked to have said to your child to take responsibility and apologise?*

## 4. Offering a reparative experience

Reparative experiences are a key part of the repair. How this looks will depend on the child. For younger children, a matching power-reversal game might be the repair that we choose. So, if we spoke loudly, the power-reversal repair might be them shouting and us jumping in the air with mock surprise each time they do. When they get to be the powerful one in the scenario, we are supporting them in repairing where they felt powerless and we used power-over them. They can move through any fight-flight response back into a sense of power. For older children, you might ask if they want to redo the whole situation, this time with how you would love to respond. You might also ask them what they'd really like to hear from you or what they would like to do.

## Children know how to heal, so asking them for ideas for the reparative experience can often bring powerful and surprising ideas to light.

*Invitation for Reflection: What do you think would have been a reparative experience at that time?*

# Repairing with Our Children After a Long Time Has Passed

As you're reading this, we wonder if you remember things that you want to repair from years ago. Another wonderful thing about Aware Parenting is that repair can happen after many years. We can really trust the timing around this. When we are ready, and our child is ready, we might find a situation presents itself, and we clearly see that this is reparative for the past experience. For example, if a parent did controlled crying with their baby, and now their child is five and they want to sleep in the parents' bed. The parent could say yes, and if the child cries in the middle of the night like a baby, this time they can hold them and listen, and say the things to that little inner baby that they wish they had said back then.

Lael says:

> When I had my first child, I had such a challenging birth experience. My first two years of motherhood felt very disconnected. I found my son challenging. Although I met all his physical needs, I was so traumatised I wasn't very present or attuned to him.
>
> As he grew, our relationship also grew, but it wasn't until he was ten years old that he brought a reparative experience to me. We were at my in-law's house playing in the pool, and all the family and cousins were around. Everyone went inside to get lunch, and it was just my son and me in the pool. He swam over to me and started talking in a baby voice and started saying things like ... 'I'm your little baby. Hold me like a baby,' and he kept wanting to snuggle into me and get me to hold him like a baby. I followed his lead and held him like a baby and started saying things to him like, 'You are my beautiful baby, and I see you, and I am here with you.' I found myself saying sorry for the times I couldn't be present, and he kept giggling and wanting to snuggle into me.
>
> He then asked me to hold his head while he floated in the water in front of me. He went very quiet and closed his eyes and floated for about five

*minutes in front of me. I had tears streaming down my face as I could feel the repair and forgiveness happening at this moment.*

*I realised that I was no longer carrying guilt for how I was when he was little, I had done the work to forgive myself and trust our experience, and here he was ten years later, completing the healing.*

*After five minutes of holding my son in the water, he opened his eyes, kissed me on the cheek and said, 'Thanks, Mum,' and then jumped out of the pool to join the rest of the family.*

*It was a deeply moving and healing experience and showed me that it is never too late to heal or repair wounds that may be there.*

## Helping Children Repair with Others

Children find it very hard to apologise when they are still upset or experience not being heard. Asking a child to say sorry when they don't feel sorry doesn't help anyone. The child will apologise to please the adult but won't really feel what they are saying. Listening to a child's feelings first and helping them feel heard in relation to the situation will help them return to their state of balance, which is more likely to lead to a genuine repair.

After a child has been heard and feels connected again, you can invite them to repair when they want to and in a way that feels right for them. Sometimes this can be a hug, using words to apologise, drawing a picture, making something for someone or offering to help or play to restore the connection. However, children who are very reluctant to repairing or apologising may have a big build up of feelings related to powerlessness or of being treated unfairly that stops them from moving into empathy and repair.

## Compassion in Parenting and Reparenting

As we discussed above, genuinely repairing with our children requires compassion and empathy for ourselves. Our mantra to parents is always to invite them to be more compassionate with themselves.

We have been so conditioned to berate ourselves and have been taught to pick up those sticks of guilt, shame, and judgement of ourselves. Your inner dialogue might be, 'I am not good enough. I am a bad parent.' But we are all doing whatever we can do in any moment. We are all walking around with unhealed trauma and unexpressed feelings. If we are willing to grow and learn, this means there will always be things we know now that we didn't know before. We invite you to replace the harsh critical voice with one of deep compassion. We don't yell at our babies when they are learning to walk and fall over – we support them to keep going. We can do the same for ourselves. When we act from anger or hurt, we are still learning, and when we give ourselves compassion instead of punishment, we create more space for healing. The more compassion we can have for ourselves, the more compassion we have for others.

So if this book has helped you connect with painful feelings, we invite you to be compassionate with yourself. Are you willing to give yourself some empathy and look to moving forward and parenting with some new skills and understanding?

*Invitation for Reflection: Would you like to write a letter to yourself back in the past when you didn't parent in a way you wanted and offer yourself compassionate understanding?*

## Our Relationship to Self-care

As you'll explore in the next chapter, we will be inviting you to feel into your own hurts to assist with your healing, which will support you to become a more present parent.

A very important factor in being able to be the parent we want to be comes down to meeting our own needs first. Self-care is a phrase thrown around a lot these days and means different things to different people. It is interesting to explore our unique relationship to self-care as we have found that, particularly for mothers, our imprints in relation to self-care are often connected to what we witnessed in our family of origin as well as the collective voice of society, which often tells us to put our needs last.

Many parents say they can't have self-care because they believe it is too hard to make it happen. We appreciate that this can be true. The lack of community and family support and financial pressures often mean that parents are juggling work and family with little reprieve. However, we have also discovered that for many parents, their relationship to creating self-care is also often linked to belief systems about meeting their needs. Many mothers we have worked with share that watching their mother sacrifice everything to take care of the family led them to believe that this is what a 'good' mother does. Women often believe that if they have time for themselves, that would mean they are selfish, or they would pick up those guilt sticks, so they just don't do it.

When we want to parent with awareness, sacrificing our own needs to meet our child's often breeds resentment and exhaustion, which makes empathic listening and playful connection almost impossible. If you identify with this, you are not alone. Over the years, we have worked with many parents who deeply align with the philosophies we have shared but often hit roadblocks due to not meeting their own needs first. As the old saying goes, 'fit your oxygen mask first, so you can then assist your child.'

*We invite you to lean into your relationship with self-care.*

- Do you carry a story that it's just too hard to get help?
- Do you think you would be selfish if you met your needs?
- Do you find it hard to ask for help?
- Do you think asking for help means that there is something wrong with you?

- Where do those stories stem from?
- What belief systems pop up when you think about meeting your needs?
- What small steps can you take to change your story in relation to self-care?

*Self-care can be many things. Doing a yoga class, talking to an empathy buddy, doing some journaling, going for a run, having a nap, anything that fills up your cup and meets your physical and emotional needs.*

We have both experienced the power of meeting our needs first so we can hold space for our children in the way we really want. In fact, we both know that the more we take care of our own needs, the more we have to offer our children. We invite you to explore this relationship to take care of yourself. We believe it is one of the critical components in parenting with empathy and compassion.

CHAPTER 10

# Exploring Our Imprints

Lael shares:

*Kate was a regular client and was open to looking at her relationship with her children. She was adamant that she wanted to parent differently than how she was raised. She often shared that her childhood wasn't terrible – it was just that her parents didn't know what to do when she got upset. They had a no-nonsense vibe in the house. Whether something was unfair or she felt sad, her mother would purse her lips and frown. Her mother was very proud that she could make her children quiet by giving them 'the look'.*

*Kate came to the session concerned that she was getting angry in response to her three-year-old daughter. She shared that her big feelings often came out of the blue, 'I was calm and listening, and then Tilly took so long to put her shoes on and get in the car, and I just lost it. The other day I ended up yelling at her, "Why won't you just hurry up!"' Kate's tears started flowing as she tells this story. 'What kind of mother am I if I yell at my daughter to get in the car. I am such a bad mum.'*

*This is a story we have heard many times before. A parent who is generally calm, and then a small thing happens, and they go from zero to a hundred on the rage scale. Often a clue into why we have big reactions has to do with our upbringing and, in particular, how we were responded to as a child. I asked Kate to tell me more about how she feels when her daughter takes a long time to do something.*

*She said, 'I feel frustrated, and if we don't get somewhere on time, I think* it's rude, and I don't want to be rude. I have this tense feeling in my body and these thoughts, "just hurry up, come on," and then I get frustrated.'

I asked Kate if she could remember what it was like being three and if she was ever rushed to do things. Kate's eyes started to well up. 'My mother rushed us for everything. And she would yell. She would yell so much that my sister and I would panic. I tried to hurry my sister as much as possible as she was much slower than me.'

I ask her if that feeling of panic she remembers as a child is similar to the feeling she gets now when her daughter is taking too long? Kate bows her head and says quietly, 'It's exactly the same.'

I asked Kate if she would be willing to share with me what she wished she could have said to her mum in those moments when she was yelling or rushing her. Without missing a beat, Kate says, 'I'm doing my best. Can't you see Mum that I am doing my best?' At this stage, Kate sobs quietly, and the tears that weren't expressed as a child start to flow.

After Kate's tears finished, we looked at the parallels between her childhood and the current reality. She makes the link between thinking she wasn't good enough in her mother's eyes ('I am doing my best!') and the thought she has a parent ('I'm not a good enough mother'). She can see that her daughter taking her time helps her connect with the same feelings of panic and fear she felt as a child. We discuss ways to support the younger parts that need to be heard and how she would have liked to be responded to by her mother. The phrases she would have liked to hear she is now going to say to her daughter.

Kate checked in with me a few weeks later and shared that the panic around being on time or rushing her daughter had dissipated. She told me that it is easy for her to be playful now when her daughter takes a long time, and in those moments of connection with her daughter, any *sense of panic disappears. The present-day response to her daughter of empathy and kindness was healing the painful feelings from the past. And, as an added bonus, 'My daughter doesn't seem to take as long doing things these days. I actually don't even mind if she does.'*

## Our Thoughts, Needs and Feelings

The suggestions in this chapter come from a collective forty-five years of our own healing journeys and the different modalities we've experienced over that time. We believe they are a wonderful complement to all that Aware Parenting offers, and we invite you to choose what feels right for you as you explore your relationship with your past and present.

Earlier on, we looked at children's behaviour and how it is affected by what they are thinking, needing and feeling, and in this chapter, we talk about how our behaviour is affected by those three things too.

If we are yelling or being reactive, permissive, judgemental, or tempted to reward, punish or run away, those behaviours invite us to look at what is happening underneath. Just as we invited you to look beneath your child's behaviour to their thoughts, needs and feelings. When we see our reactive behaviour as an invitation to explore our own story or themes, parenting becomes a journey of self-discovery rather than a recurring struggle.

Sometimes our reactions can shift once we have new information (perhaps coming to read a chapter of this book), and sometimes by meeting needs for support, rest or empathy. Still, at other times they can be an invitation to heal past hurts. If we want to change our parenting, we generally need to address all three of these causes of our behaviour.

## 1. What We Are Thinking/What We Believe/What We Understand

The first cause is what we are thinking or what information we have, but it's also about our core beliefs.

Lael uses the word 'imprint' to refer to the belief systems we took on board as a child about how the world works. Every one of us has different imprints that we were conditioned with. These are the thoughts we had in response to what we experienced in our family. For example, if we grew up in a family where our parents modelled to us through their words and actions that 'you can't trust anyone in the world, people are always out there to rip you off,' you may have developed an imprint that said 'the world is not safe. I can't trust anyone,' as that is the story that was told over and over again at home. These imprints often shape the way we look at life and how we interact with the world.

Our imprints are belief systems that we look through to reinforce that these are true. Someone who grew up in a family with a message in relation to trust that said, 'You can always trust your intuition to guide you, and people are there to support and help you,' will then look for that evidence. Our imprints are the stories we take on board as children, and we don't often question them until we come across adversity, become a parent or find challenges in intimate relationships. And it is often through the child's lens that we create the story, so as adults, what we believe and what we look for is often through the eyes of a child.

In this chapter, we will be inviting you to explore your own imprints. The beauty of this exploration is that when we understand the beliefs and imprints we acquired growing up, we see that we have the power to change because these ways of thinking are not 'just the way things are.' As children, we believe these to be true. As adults, we have a choice about whether we are willing to continue believing that we can never have support, be loved, be understood, or live the life we want. These core beliefs or imprints can be changed, partly through experiencing new experiences.

*Core beliefs/imprints can take time to change, AND it is possible to change them, not only for ourselves but also for our children*

## 2. What We Need

The second cause of our parenting behaviour is our needs. As parents, when our needs are unmet, and particularly when they are chronically unmet, attending to our children's needs and feelings becomes very hard. Have you ever tried to offer attachment play or a Loving Limit when you haven't received any empathy from another adult for ages or when you are tired from lack of sleep or need some acknowledgement and appreciation for all that you're doing? This is naturally going to be hard. This is because, as we talked about in Chapter 2, when we have unmet needs, our body is literally alerting us to meet that need by sending uncomfortable sensations.

Being willing to take action to meet your needs will profoundly affect how you feel in your body and how much available attention you have to attend to your child's needs and feelings. Yet, that is a big journey in itself. As we've discussed, what Marion calls the 'Disconnected Domination Culture' has trained most of us to ignore or judge our needs. As mothers, many of us learnt that mothers don't have needs, or if we do, that those needs are at the bottom of the list. Most of us will need to do inner work to change our beliefs about our needs so that we are actually willing to meet them.

## 3. What We're Feeling

The third cause of our parenting behaviour is our feelings. Most of our painful parenting moments will generally come from our own painful feelings, most often from our own experiences as children. When we feel big and overwhelming feelings with our children, such as powerlessness, fear, or rage, this generally tells us that our feelings from the past are showing up.

In fact, that's often one of the signs that these are feelings from the past; they are overwhelming and all-consuming and seem as if they have always been there and will go on forever. Sometimes just knowing that these feelings are from the past and are showing up to be heard now can help us feel less overwhelmed by them.

In many sessions with parents, we have seen a child's behaviour shift and change as soon as a parent acknowledges their own past experiences of hurt. As they bring awareness and healing to those parts from the past, the child's behaviour often changes or resolves, sometimes without the parent even changing what they are doing.

We have come to believe that our children are our wise teachers. They bring to the surface all the parts of us that need to be healed so we are less likely to pass on our emotional hurts and themes down to them. Often their behaviours or challenges are invitations to explore our own feelings, so the child doesn't have any extra baggage to carry forward. This supports our children to be freer to be who they really are.

When we understand this as parents, we will generally find it easier to look behind the behaviour and not move into blame or punishment in response to what our children are doing. Instead, we can ask, 'What is going on for me in this scenario and is there something for me to listen to?'

The more we understand and bring healing to our own story and themes, the less reactive we will be to our children. The more reparenting we do, the more we can parent our children in ways that we are called to.

To raise our children as consciously as we can, both pieces of the puzzle are required:

1. What is going on for my child? – What are they thinking, needing and feeling?
2. What is going on for me? – What am I thinking, needing and feeling?

If we can meet our children with empathy, play, openness and Limits or Loving Limits where called for, we are offering a safe and compassionate environment so that they can be themselves and heal from hurts as they move through life.

You may also find that some big feelings may arise in relation to your parents or caregivers as you explore your past. This is a normal and natural part of the process. We have both found that as this journey continues and more feelings are expressed, people tend to develop deep compassion for themselves as well as their parents.

Remember that historical and cultural piece to this work? When we look at the time and culture each generation was born in, we are more likely to be able to feel compassion for their responses. Perhaps you might even consider how you would have parented had you been born at the time your parents had. People often think that they can only be compassionate towards themselves OR their parents. Part of this work is, in our own natural timing, feeling compassion for ourselves and then compassion for our parents. As our unheard feelings get to be felt, expressed and heard, we can more clearly see things through the eyes of our parents and the experiences they had growing up, as well as the information that was available to them at the time. The more we can be with the younger parts of us who experienced painful feelings, the more we can see and understand how those people in our past acted in those painful ways.

As we learn to see behind our child/ren's behaviour, and tune in to their thoughts, needs and feelings, and as we can do that for ourselves, so we can see that behind those behaviours which had such painful impacts on us as children, our parents and caretakers who acted in those ways were also carrying painful cultural ways of thinking, unmet needs, and their own past hurts.

Having an empathy buddy can be a core part of this healing process. An empathy buddy is another adult who understands these concepts and who is willing to be lovingly present with you as you explore your feelings and in turn you listen to them in the same way. An empathy buddy is not there to offer advice, but to just listen and hold space for your feelings and thoughts. Being heard by another adult allows us to feel and express our own feelings so we have more spaciousness within ourselves to provide a welcoming space for our child's feelings.

## Aware Parenting and Our Inner Work

In attending to these feelings, we have ways of working with parents that, although they don't directly come from Aletha Solter, are inspired by Aware Parenting and are deeply complementary. Aware Parenting certainly invites you to attend to your own past. For example, at the end of each chapter of *The Aware Baby*, Aletha Solter invites you to reflect on your own experiences growing up. In our work, we expand on this. We find that whenever parents can make links between their own behaviour and feelings and their child's, more understanding and compassion arrive. For that reason, we will be inviting you to attend to the same topics in yourself that we went through for children.

You may feel comfortable reading some of the sections and questions below, and you might feel uncomfortable when reading others. When we look at how we were raised, it is completely understandable that we might have big feelings showing up in certain places. For example, a child who grew up with a great deal of yelling and aggression might come to view that as a normal way of communicating or may swing in the other direction and have big feelings of terror or powerlessness arise whenever there is a conflict with their child.

*We invite you to be compassionate with yourself as you delve into this deeper exploration.*

Marion says:

*We also remind you to listen to your willingness at every step. We invite you to not coerce yourself into exploring things. Your psyche knows exactly what you are ready to work with and will let you know if you're not quite ready. If you suddenly feel tired or distracted, or you just don't want to do it, please listen. You can always come back another time when you are willing to. Listening to our willingness can be a powerful part of our healing from when we were forced to do things as children.*

## Invitation for Reparenting

Lael says:

*Here is a series of question prompts for inner reparenting from me. If you want to do more after that, Marion will add some invitations from her Inner Loving Presence Process work. We invite you to write the answers down – often, the experience is way more powerful when we journal about something rather than just answer the questions in our minds. You'll notice that the topics parallel those we went through in the book.*

### *Suppression and Addiction*

- What was the imprint of this for you?
- What did your parents do to protect themselves from feelings? (Smoking, drinking, working too much, etc.)
- What was modelled to you at times when things were stressful?
- How did your parents behave when they were stressed?
- What generational imprints can you identify as being handed down regarding repressing feelings or addictions?
- How does this play out for you now?
- What is your go-to repression for when you don't want to feel?
- When do you use it the most?
- What is it protecting you from feeling?
- Do you recognise this story with your own child?
- Can you identify what your child's key ways of repressing are?
- Is it similar to yours? (For example, do you both become extra busy, or do you want to use technology, or do you want to eat more food?)
- What feelings surface for you when you see your child using repression?
- What did you need that you didn't get?

- As a child, what did you use as your repression, and what did you need from your parents then?
- What did you wish your parents had modelled for you around expressing feelings?

What do you want the imprint to be for yourself moving forward? For example – 'It is safe for me to feel all my emotions, and I can trust myself to call in all the support I need.'

## *Cooperation/Not Listening*

- What was the imprint of this for you?
- Were you told what to do and expected to do it?
- Were you frequently told that you 'had' to do things?
- What happened if you questioned what was asked of you?
- Were your feelings or instincts overridden by the adults around you?
- Did your parents have a hard time setting limits with you? Did they plead or beg you to just 'do the right thing'?
- Were you punished or shamed if you didn't do what the adults asked you to do?
- How does this play out for you now?
- Do you find yourself doing things that you don't want to do but believe you 'should' do?
- Do you worry about people feeling upset if you don't do what they ask?
- Do you feel big feelings bubble up when people tell you what to do?
- What is your belief system around this now? (For example, 'I must do what others want me to do to stay safe' or 'Nobody can tell me what to do.') Do you recognise this story with your own child?
- What feelings surface for you when you think that your child isn't listening or cooperating?

- Do you resort to power-over when your child won't do what you ask?
- Do you find it hard to set a Loving Limit if your child is behaving in a way that is challenging?
- If your child doesn't want to do what you ask, do you give in and let them do what they want?
- Do you feel powerless when your child says no or isn't willing to cooperate?
- What did you need that you didn't get?
- Thinking back to your childhood, what did you need to be able to listen to your feelings or thoughts around cooperation and not listening?
- What did you want from your parents or caregivers around cooperation and giving you choice and autonomy?

What do you want the imprint to be for yourself moving forward? For example: 'It is safe for me to speak my truth and be heard.' 'I have choice and autonomy in my life, and I am loved and respected for it.'

## *Feelings/Tantrums*

- What was the imprint of this for you?
- Was it safe for you to cry or rage?
- What happened in your family when you were upset or scared?
- Was your crying welcomed?
- Were your frustrations and rage welcomed?
- Were you labelled as 'too emotional' or 'sensitive'?
- Did your parent or caregiver try and fix everything when you were upset?
- What was the message in your house around big feelings?
- How does this play out for you now?
- Do you feel uncomfortable when children or adults express emotions?

- Do you get angry or upset when someone is releasing big feelings?
- Do you jump to fix or solve problems when someone is upset?
- Do you try to repress your feelings?
- Do you recognise this story with your own child?
- How do you respond when your child is upset or angry?
- Do you move to shut it down, fix it, or distract them?
- Can you be with their big feelings?
- What do you observe that your child does when they have big feelings?
- Do they express, suppress or move into aggression? Is that similar to what you do?
- What did you need that you didn't get?
- If you think back to your own childhood, what was it that you needed when it came to your expression of big feelings?
- What did you want to hear from your parents or caregivers when upset?

What do you want the imprint to be for yourself moving forward? For example – 'It is safe for me to express all my feelings' or 'All parts of me are loved and supported.'

## *Aggression/Power-Over*

- What was the imprint of this for you?
- How was anger navigated in your house growing up?
- Did you have to hide/shut down/be 'good' when one of your caregivers was angry?
- Were yelling and aggression a normal part of your childhood?
- Were anger and rage channelled and expressed in safe ways?
- Did your parents/caregivers resort to power-over when things didn't go the way they wanted them to?

- How does this play out for you now?
- Are you uncomfortable when you see or experience frustration, anger or rage?
- Do you find yourself getting angry whenever you feel powerless?
- Do you play 'small' or be 'good' to try to stop someone from getting angry?
- Do you struggle to set Loving Limits because you don't want people to be upset?
- Do you recognise this story with your own child?
- Does your child mirror your behaviour and beliefs around anger?
- Do you need to control and power-over your child whenever you feel powerless?
- Since becoming a parent, have you felt rage and anger in a way you never have before as an adult?
- Do you try to appease your child, so they don't get angry?
- What did you need that you didn't get?
- If you think back to your own childhood, what was it that you needed when it came to anger being expressed?
- What did you want to hear from your parents or caregivers when you were angry?
- What did you wish you could have expressed or said to the adults in your life about their anger and power-over?

What do you want the imprint to be for yourself moving forward? For example: 'It is safe for me to express all my anger and rage, and I am willing to heal and support the feelings that sit beneath it' or 'All parts of me are loved and supported.'

## *Fear/Anxiety/Trust/Attachment and Separation*

- What was the imprint of this for you?
- What belief system was passed onto you around trust?
- Were your parents/caregivers anxious when you were younger – how did you feel when you could sense their fear?
- What was your imprint around separation?
- Was it safe for you to be in the world?
- Did you have a healthy attachment with your parents/caregivers?
- Was your relationship with your parent/s enmeshed – did one or both of your parents live through you?
- How does this play out for you now?
- Do you find it hard to trust life?
- Do you struggle with limits with your parents or family members?
- Do you find it easy to trust your intuition and inner guidance as an adult?
- Do you recognise this story with your own child?
- Do you find it hard to navigate separation with your child?
- Do you feel scared to let your child be in the world?
- Do you often worry or feel fearful when you think about your child?
- Can you trust your child's unique journey?
- What did you need that you didn't get?
- If you think back to your own childhood, what was it that you needed when it came to trusting yourself?
- What did you want to hear from your parents or caregivers around life and following your own path?
- What do you want the Imprint to be for yourself moving forward? For example – 'It is safe for me to trust my intuition and inner guidance. I am willing to be supported in living my life to the fullest, and I am loved and celebrated for doing so.'

## *Sleep*

- What was the imprint of this for you?
- Was sleeping a challenge when you were growing up?
- Were you left alone to cry?
- Did you feel fearful sleeping on your own?
- Were you expected to get into bed and go straight to sleep even if you weren't tired?
- Was sleep a wonderful imprint with lots of closeness, love and support?
- How does this play out for you now?
- Do you find it hard to fall asleep/stay asleep?
- Do you need something at night to help you go to sleep?
- Do you generally do something right before sleep?
- Do you struggle with feelings that surface at nighttime?
- Do you recognise this story with your own child?
- Has sleep become a stressful dynamic in your family?
- Do you have a lot of feelings that arise when your children won't sleep or struggle to get to sleep?
- Did you/do you use similar techniques with your child that were used with you when you were younger to go to sleep?
- What did you need that you didn't get?
- Thinking back to your childhood, what did you need when it came to sleep and feeling safe?
- What did you wish your parents had said or done around sleep when you were young?

What do you want the imprint to be for yourself moving forward? For example – 'I trust my child's ability and my own to sleep deeply. We have all we need to support our bodies to have restful and rejuvenating experiences.'

If you want to continue diving deeper, Marion will share some elements from her Inner Loving Presence Process.

## The Inner Loving Presence Process

Marion says:

*Remember in Aware Parenting that children need the loving presence of us as adults to listen to their feelings to make the expression healing rather than traumatising? For healing to happen as adults, we generally either need an outer loving listener, or an internal loving presence.*

*Your outer loving listener can be an empathy buddy, a therapist or counsellor, or an Aware Parenting instructor.*

I have developed 'The Inner Loving Presence Process', in which we do the equivalent of what we are doing with our children when we are practising Aware Parenting, but this time with our inner child from our Inner Loving Parents. We can go through the Inner Loving Presence Process questions with an empathy buddy, and over time we develop relationships with our Inner Loving Parents and can go through the process with them.

The first step is to connect with an Inner Loving Parent figure, which is a sense of connecting with a compassionate inner presence.

Before you go any further, I invite you to check in with whether you are willing to explore feelings and experiences from your past and to connect with younger parts of you. If you are already feeling immersed in big feelings, overwhelmed or flooded, or you've got really big things going on in your life at the moment, I recommend not going any further. If you have a yes to continuing, I invite you to tune in to how deep you want to go. You can connect with the earlier experiences in more of a cognitive way, or you can go all the way in and identify with those younger parts of you, literally revisiting an experience of the past. Again, I wouldn't recommend identifying with a younger part if you tend to get flooded by feelings or if you tend to dissociate or get scared by your feelings. The earlier back you go, the more likely you will need outer loving listening.

If you have a yes to continue, here is some of the **Inner Loving Presence Process:**

1. I invite you to either have someone who meets your need for empathy listen to your responses or connect with a felt sense of loving presence within, which might be your Inner Loving Mother or Inner Loving Father. This kind of emotional healing requires the younger parts of us to know that we are not alone with the feelings this time and are being lovingly supported. You might want to put your arms around your shoulders or your hand on your heart and hear the phrase, 'I'm here with you'.

2. When your child does something that you react to, do you notice a charged phrase? (A charged phrase is something you think or say that has a lot of emotional charge for you. It might be, 'He never listens to me' or, 'Why don't you ever do what I ask?' Or it might be that your child says, 'NO!' and you feel rage bubbling inside. Whenever the feelings are out of proportion to the present situation, we know there are feelings from the past that are coming up to be heard.) Would you like to share this phrase with your inner or outer loving presence? They might say, 'I hear how upset you feel when he doesn't listen to you/they don't do what you ask/when she says no.'

There are two ways you can go with the next step, which is designed to help you connect with where the feelings originate.

a) Does this remind you of something from your past?

or b) How old do you feel?

3. Again, you can invite your outer or inner loving presence to listen to that experience. You might have a vague sense of some theme in your life, you might remember a repeated feeling or thought, or you might

have a particular memory. Or you might not really have any of these but just have a sense that these feelings and thoughts are familiar somehow. There is no right or wrong way to do this, so whichever way you feel a sense of the feelings from the past, please go with that way!

4. How did / do you feel? As that younger person, how did you feel? If you want to go in more immersively to the experience, the question is, 'how do you feel?' so that you are literally re-visiting the feelings from the past. Again, please only do this if you feel a lot of presence for your feelings! The inner or outer loving presence hears and gives empathy, 'I hear that you feel …' You could use the two-column technique, where the younger part of you expresses feelings on the left side of a piece of paper and the Inner Loving Presence offers compassion on the right! Five-year-old-you: 'I feel frustrated.' Inner Loving Mother: 'I hear that you feel frustrated. I'm here and I'm listening. I welcome your frustration.' Five-year-old you: 'I feel REALLY frustrated!' Inner Loving Mother: 'I really hear that you're really frustrated. I'm here with you. I'm listening.' Keep going until you feel a sigh of relief, and a deep sense of being heard.

5. What did / do you think? Repeat the same process from step 4, again experiencing being deeply heard. Five-year-old-you: 'I think that you don't love me.' Inner Loving Mother: 'Oh sweetheart, I really hear that you think I don't love you. I'm here. I'm listening.'

6. What did / do you need? Again with compassionate listening to the response! Five-year-old you: 'I need reassurance that you do love me.' Inner Loving Mother: 'Of course you need reassurance that I do love you, sweetheart.'

7. What did you need to say or do? What do you need to say or do? With a loving listening to the response! Five-year-old-you: I need to come up close to you and cling on to you and say, 'PLEASE tell me that you love me, Mummy.' Inner Loving Mother: 'Sweetheart, I'm here with you as you do that. I really hear that you want me to tell you that I love you.'

8. What did you need to hear or experience? What do you need to hear

or experience? Again, with an empathic response until you feel relief. Five-year-old you: 'I want you to put your arms around me and say, "I'm so sorry that you thought I didn't love you. I so understand how frustrated and hurt you felt. I'm here. I love you. I have always loved you and I will always love you." Inner Loving Mother puts her arms around you and says, 'I'm so sorry that you thought I didn't love you. I so understand how frustrated and hurt you felt. I'm here. I love you. I have always loved you and I will always love you.'

9. What would present-day you like to tell past you about how your life unfolded and changed since that time in the past? e.g. 'Five-year-old me, because of your experience of thinking you weren't loved, I have made sure that I tell my children every day that I love them. I give them lots of cuddles and closeness and I check in with them that they really feel my love. Your experience wasn't in vain. It made a difference.'

This process can bring profound healing to our experiences from the past when we didn't get to feel, express or receive what we needed. This time we get to feel the feelings, express them, which might include crying and raging, and receive the loving listening and support we need.

Just as with Aware Parenting, a child getting to feel and express their feelings whilst being heard by an adult who is present with them gets to heal from that experience, so with the Inner Loving Presence Process, our younger parts get to have their feelings, thoughts and needs heard, and receive a reparative experience of what they needed to say and do, and hear and receive, which brings healing and relief. In this way, we become increasingly freed from repetitive themes that we otherwise keep experiencing again and again, which are invitations to heal all along.

# Conclusion

**Compassion and Willingness to Heal**

We wonder how are you feeling now, having read this book? We are so willing for you to have an even greater understanding about the true causes of both your child's behaviour and feelings, as well as your own. Not only that, we invite you to keep dropping those guilt sticks and choosing compassion for yourself and the unique path your parenting has taken.

As you explore new concepts and try out different ways of responding to your children, you might feel confused, daunted, overwhelmed or unsure. We invite you to keep listening in to what resonates with you, putting it into practice, and observing your child/ren's behaviour for evidence that this is helpful for them. You are the authority in your parenting, and creating an observational experimental practice will help you gain information about what is helpful and what is not, so you can move forwards in your parenting with increasing reassurance and confidence.

Changing intergenerational patterns can take time, so we encourage you to be gentle with yourself and reach out for support whenever possible. There are many wonderful Aware Parenting instructors all over the world who work with these principles and practices and can often support. You can find a list of them at **www.awareparenting.com/instruct.htm**. If you are looking for an Aware Parenting instructor in Australia or New Zealand, you can find them on Marion's website **www.marionrose.net**.

We also encourage you to connect with an empathy buddy who can provide a safe place to be heard and who can offer the support and compassion that is vital when it comes to healing from our own childhood hurts and conditioning that is required when we practice Aware Parenting. There is a Facebook group called Aware Parenting Listening Partners where you can reach out for one. (Listening Partners is a term created by Hand in Hand Parenting and is often borrowed in Aware Parenting.)

We also invite you to go slowly. Much like we shared in this book about trusting children's timing to heal, we also trust our own timing as adults to heal past hurts. As your child/ren grow you may find that different stages of their development remind you of events and circumstances in your own life when you were that age. Sometimes we don't have to go looking for the parts that need healing – they will just present themselves. This is a gentle reminder to stay open and trust the process of healing your past so you can create the future you desire.

Thank you for reading our book. We are both deeply passionate about creating a more compassionate world for children and we believe that starts with more love, acceptance and compassion for all feelings and the deep understanding of how feelings cause behaviour.

You are part of creating that world. Together, we really can help children become the compassionate and resilient adults they were born to be, deeply connected with themselves and equipped with the true power they need to create change in the world.

# Glossary

## Aware Parenting Terminology

**Attachment play:** Nine specific kinds of play between parents and children as described in Aletha Solter's book *Attachment Play*. This type of play creates connection, cooperation, and supports children to both prepare for, and heal from, stressful or traumatic events.

**Balance of attention:** A state in which a child feels emotionally safe while being reminded of a trauma. A balance of attention is necessary for emotional release and healing to occur through crying, playing or laughter.

**Control pattern:** Repetitive or compulsive behaviours which are usually acquired during infancy and childhood to suppress crying and strong emotions. A typical control pattern is thumb-sucking. Control patterns can put babies and children into states of mind dissociation. They are also called emotional suppression habits and self-soothing behaviours.

**Crying-in-arms approach:** The practice of holding babies while they cry (after all their needs are met) and communicating love, empathy and reassurance.

**Limits:** Limits are when a parent expresses their 'no' to their child when they aren't willing to do something, or for something to happen. These are flexible and temporary because they express what the parent is not willing for in that moment. For example, when a parent isn't willing to take their child to the park because they are feeling tired.

**Loving Limits:** The combination of a verbal or physical limit with empathy to create a pretext for a child to cry to release pent-up stress. Loving Limits say no to a behaviour and yes to the underlying feelings causing the behaviour. (This term was developed by Marion and adopted by Aletha Solter.) This is different to Limits, which are when an adult says 'no' based on their needs and willingness rather than because of the child's behaviour and feelings.

**Emotional Release:** Any behaviour that discharges tension from the nervous system and helps restore homeostasis. Forms of emotional release in children include crying, tantrums, trembling, laughter, certain kinds of therapeutic play, and body movements. These are also called healing mechanisms and tension-release mechanisms.

## Marion's Terminology

**Charged phrase:** A phrase we often say as parents that comes from our childhood that we are projecting onto our children.

**Disconnected Domination Culture (DDC):** The culture of industrialised countries, based on disconnection and power-over. This includes parenting practices and language that create disconnection and domination.

**Emotional sticks:** Harsh judgements that we learnt from the **Disconnected Domination Culture** that we then use to hurt ourselves. Guilt, shame and self-judgement are examples of this.

**Inner Loving Presences:** Our internal loving supporters, such as our Inner Loving Mother and Inner Loving Father, who are present with us when we need them, who can be with all of our feelings, who love us unconditionally and who offer us reparative experiences for our childhood. They help us reparent ourselves, using the knowledge and practices of Aware Parenting.

**Inner Loving Presence Process:** This is a process we can go through with the support of our Inner Loving Presences, to revisit the past and create healing there.

**Parenting mantra:** An easy-to-remember phrase that we consciously choose to replace our cultural conditioning about children. For example, 'He's not doing this deliberately. He's not enjoying this. He needs my help.'

**Power-over:** This is when we use our greater physical, emotional, cognitive or economic power to coerce our children into doing things they are not willing to do.

**Reparative experiences:** Experiences which create healing because they were what we wanted to happen the first time around and which meet our needs for empathy, acknowledgement, understanding and more.

**Reparenting:** This is when we use Aware Parenting to parent our own inner children, responding to them the way we would our 'outer' children.

**Themes:** Patterns that can be observed in our lives, often beginning at birth and early childhood. We keep repeating the themes because the younger parts of us want to have our feelings heard and to experience reparative experiences.

**Willingness:** Different to wanting to do something or doing something because we are either being forced to or are forcing ourselves; willingness is a full-bodied 'yes'.

**Younger parts:** Like our inner child, these parts of us have unexpressed feelings to share with us. When we are in a younger part, we feel and think as we did at that age.

## Lael's Terminology

**Holding Space:** This is when we are feeling calm and centred and we create a safe space for a child (or adult) to share their feelings and thoughts. This often involves being present, listening and trusting what is being expressed. It doesn't involve fixing or trying to make things better or jumping in with your own story of relating to how they feel. Holding space is simply being present with someone's upset feelings and offering them loving empathy and compassion.

**Imprints:** The stories and belief systems that we take on board as a child that colour our perception of the world.

**In balance:** When we are feeling centred and relaxed in our being.

**Look behind the behaviour:** Understanding that there is always a reason for any behaviour.

**Out of balance:** When we have a build-up of feelings or needs not being met.

**Spaciousness:** Our ability to stay present and open in relationship when we are listening.

## Our Favourite Phrases for Challenging Moments

### *When They're Upset*

- 'I'm here with you.'
- 'I'm listening.'
- 'I see that you're upset.'
- 'I will stay right here with you.'
- 'You're letting it all out.'
- 'I welcome all of your feelings.'

Marion says:

> *'I love all these same phrases for our inner reparenting. For example, Our Inner Loving Mother can say all of these to us.'*

### *Loving Limits*

- 'I hear that you want me to read you another book, sweetie, and I'm not willing to read any more. And I'm here and I'm listening.'
- 'I'm not willing for you to hit Susan, sweetheart, and I'm right here and I'm listening.'

## Reminders for Challenging Moments

Children don't want to do things that we find annoying. When they're behaving in challenging ways, they either need information, have unmet needs, or have painful feelings.

We can:

1. Give them information.
2. Meet their needs for connection and choice.
3. Make things fun or listen to their upset feelings.

## *When Your Child is Suppressing Feelings*

1. Avoid judging yourself or them.
2. Move in with warm connection.
3. Offer relevant attachment play.
4. Offer a Loving Limit.

## *Reducing Aggression in Your Child*

1. Offer plenty of choices.
2. Avoid using power-over.
3. Offer nondirective child-centred play and power-reversal games.
4. Respond to aggression with attachment play or Loving Limits.

## *When Your Child's Using a Screen*

1. Reach a mutual agreement regarding screen time.
2. Give them a gentle reminder about that agreement.
3. Come in and connect before that time.
4. Support the transition, e.g. with attachment play.
5. Offer a Loving Limit if necessary.
6. Welcome any tears and tantrums.

# Further Resources

## The Aware Parenting Podcast

This is our podcast, which inspired this book. You can find it on all the usual podcast channels!

## Aletha Solter

If you enjoyed this book and want to learn more, we highly recommend looking at the work of the founder of Aware Parenting, Aletha Solter, PhD.

www.awareparenting.com

Books:
- The Aware Baby
- Cooperative and Connected: Helping Children Flourish without Punishments or Rewards
- Tears and Tantrums: What to Do when Babies and Children Cry
- Raising Drug-Free Kids: 100 Tips for Parents
- Attachment Play: How to Solve Children's Behavior Problems with Play, Laughter and Connection
- Healing Your Traumatized Child: A Parent's Guide to Children's Natural Recovery Processes

# Acknowledgments

We would like to thank Mike Gaal for his amazing cover design as well as his insightful understanding of what we've created. Big thanks to Katie Parker, Danni Yudelman, Tarryn Robertson, Matt Hamilton, and Joss Goulden for their feedback, suggestions and loving help with our book. We so appreciate Tracey-Kay Coe for your systemic constellations magic. We would also like to thank Hugh for his continued support and wonderful words.

We are so grateful to all the people who helped us bring this book into the world. A very big thank you to Julie Postance for all your wisdom, guidance and suggestions, Sandy Draper for your editing, Jenny Exall for your proof-reading, Marion's mum Jan for your proofreading and Sophie White for your typesetting. We send deep gratitude to Aletha Solter for your support, for creating an incredible foundation for us to stand on, as well as for proofreading the book for us.

# About the Authors

Lael Stone is an educator, TEDx speaker, author, mother, and parenting counsellor who has been working with families for over 20 years. She is the co-creator of Woodline Primary School, an innovative new school based on emotional wellbeing and connection. Lael is the co-host of The Aware Parenting Podcast and a sought-after public speaker who talks candidly about her experiences and her great passion; creating wellness in families through connection and communication. As well as sitting on a few advisory boards and consulting with organisations around emotional awareness and trauma-informed practices, she has teamed up with The Resilience Project to deliver presentations around raising resilient children all over Australia.

www.laelstone.com.au

# About the Authors

Marion Rose has been involved in studying psychology and consciousness since 1987 and has a PhD on postnatal depression and the mother-infant relationship from Cambridge University. After a decade in academia, including researching infant development as a post-Doctoral Research Fellow and teaching and supervising MA students, as well as training and working as a psychotherapist, Marion saw that a more powerful and precise way to create change was to work directly with parents in birth and parenting. Marion has been practicing Aware Parenting since 2002 and is the mother of a daughter and a son. She has been an Aware Parenting instructor since 2005 and is a Level Two instructor and the Regional Coordinator for Australia and New Zealand. Marion is also the founder of The Marion Method, which is a psychospiritual paradigm of parenting, reparenting and reculturing. She mentors people to become Aware Parenting instructors and Marion Method mentors. Marion has been creating online courses since 2014 in Aware Parenting and the Marion Method and is passionate about creating cultural change through these paradigms. As well as co-hosting The Aware Parenting Podcast with Lael, Marion also co-hosts The Aware Parenting and Natural Learning Podcast with Joss Goulden as well as hosting her own podcast, The Psychospiritual Podcast.

www.marionrose.net

www.ingramcontent.com/pod-product-compliance
Lightning Source LLC
Chambersburg PA
CBHW020320010526
44107CB00054B/1920